Praise

Positively Rare is a poignant collection of patient stories that illuminate the journey through a medical system where clarity often seems elusive. Each narrative reveals the profound struggles and unexpected triumphs of those grappling with rare and undiagnosed conditions. This book sheds light on the resilience and hope that drive individuals to seek answers despite a maze of uncertainty and fragmented care. Through these powerful accounts, *Positively Rare* offers a compelling glimpse into the human spirit's quest for understanding and healing. This book is a testament to the courage of patients and the ongoing search for solutions in an increasingly complex health care landscape.
Dr. Cornelia Griggs, pediatric surgeon and assistant professor of surgery at Harvard Medical School and author of bestseller *The Sky Was Falling*

These unapologetically honest, highly personal stories of navigating a rare illness are tied with a common thread: how the authors have not only emerged from their darkest hours but also channelled their unique experiences to enrich and find purpose in their lives. A must-read guide for people with rare illnesses and a master class in empathy for caregivers, friends, family, and medical professionals.
Dr. Tamara Maiuri, Huntington's disease researcher and published author in *Huntington's Disease Heroes*

I am thrilled to endorse *Positively Rare*, a remarkable collection of real-life stories that shed light on the experiences of individuals living with rare conditions. Illness is hard. But managing a rare condition is a completely different beast. This book is a powerful testament to the resilience, courage, and strength of those who navigate the challenges of these uncommon illnesses. Each story is a heartfelt and inspiring journey, offering invaluable insights and fostering a deeper understanding of the unique struggles faced by these individuals and their families. *Positively Rare* is an essential read for anyone seeking to broaden their perspective of living with a rare condition or yearning to feel less alone if struggling with one.
Melissa Adams, host of the *I Am Not My Pain* podcast and chronic pain fighter

The stories by authors such as Laura Will, Tessa Koller, and Adrienne Shirk in the new anthology by Erin Paterson, *Positively Rare*, are not only inspiring but also beautifully written. Finding out you or your family member has a rare disease that is little understood and usually untreatable is a devastating experience. The stories in *Positively Rare* honestly reveal deep emotions and fears, suspensefully describing the authors' journeys to build their courage and resilience as they face the ultimate challenge of living with a rare disease.
Nina Wachsman, CEO of Know Rare and Agatha-nominated author of *The Gallery of Beauties* and the Venice Beauties Mysteries

POSITIVELY RARE

EMPOWERING STORIES FROM THE RARE DISEASE COMMUNITY

POSITIVELY RARE

EMPOWERING STORIES FROM THE RARE DISEASE COMMUNITY

Foreword by Jessica Fein

Edited by Erin Paterson

Copyright © 2024,Lemonade Press
Book Club Copyright © 2024, Lemonade Press
All rights reserved. No portion of this book may be reproduced in any form whatsoever without the prior written permission of the publisher.

Ebook ISBN 978-1-7779179-5-1
Paperback ISBN 978-1-7779179-4-4

Cover design: Yana Katz

Interior design: Kate Smith

The events in this book are portrayed to the best of each writer's memory. Although it was impossible to recall exact conversations word for word, the essence of the dialogue is accurate. Some names and physical descriptions have been changed to protect the privacy of others. This book is not a substitute for medical advice. The reader should consult with their doctor for any matters related to their health.

For information about special discounts for bulk purchases, please contact the publisher. www.lemonadecommunity.com

50 percent of the profits from the sale of this book will be donated to Global Genes.

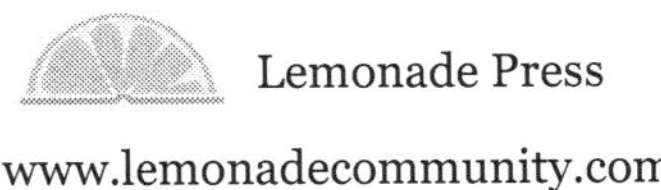

Lemonade Press

www.lemonadecommunity.com

This book is a collection of stories told by rare disease community members in their own voice, representing varied experiences of how their lives have been impacted by different rare diseases. Many of the stories contain sensitive topics that may be triggering for some people.

Topics include but are not limited to caregiving, death, depression, family planning, genetic testing, grief, hospice, medical procedures, medical trauma, post-traumatic stress disorder (PTSD), suicidal ideations, and survivor's guilt.

To help you navigate this book, we have included a list of topics for each story, allowing you to move through the book as you please based on your own personal journey and well-being. You can find this list in the Chapter Chat Topic Guide on page #171.

If at any time you need support, please know you are not alone. Many local associations are available to assist with your needs or lend a listening ear. For an international list of local resources, refer to globalgenes.org (https://globalgenes.org/mental-health-and-well-being).

50 percent of the profits from the sale of this book will be donated to our charity partner.

Table of Contents

Foreword

When my daughter Dalia was diagnosed with MERRF syndrome at age five, I had no idea what it meant.

The doctor told my husband and me that MERRF was an ultra-rare degenerative mitochondrial disease, and there wasn't enough data to predict how fast or severe the disease progression would be. He underscored that there was no curative treatment, and the only thing he could say for sure was the areas where Dalia already had symptoms would undoubtedly get worse. The fact that she was wobbly on her feet meant she'd one day rely on a wheelchair. Her mild hearing loss would become severe hearing loss.

All of it was baffling. I had a vague recollection of mitochondria from high school biology, though I couldn't begin to tell you why they were important. But it wasn't only the nature of the diagnosis that made no sense. I couldn't wrap my head around what the diagnosis would mean for my daughter, for my other children, or for my husband and me.

That evening, hours after we'd been given a life-changing decree, nothing had changed from a practical perspective. We ate dinner, we played hide-and-go-seek, we did baths and bedtime. But all the while, there was a fog that had descended. It wasn't yet a storm—just an ominous grey cloud that took up residence in our home and our hearts.

It would be months before our calendar was filled with speech therapy, physical therapy, and occupational therapy appointments;

years before Dalia lost her ability to walk, talk, and breathe without a ventilator; and more than a decade before Dalia died.

At first, my friends and extended family were as confused as I was. I sent them articles I found on Google about MERRF syndrome. But I wasn't able to share how we were doing, how I felt about the diagnosis, how Dalia was holding up. It was all a blur.

My friends didn't know how to react when I first told them the news, or in the years that followed. I couldn't blame them. I didn't know how I wanted them to react either. I didn't want to hear about their child's strep throat or sprained ankle. Relatively speaking, those were mild hiccups. But I didn't want them to feel like they had to censor themselves when talking to me. They were in a no-win situation. I tried and failed to explain the intensity of our lives, what it felt like to be on the precipice 24/7. We, too, were in a no-win situation.

My family became increasingly isolated as Dalia's disease progressed. The only people who truly understood what our lives were like were the caregivers who spent hours in our home each week. They had front-row seats to the fear, the anguish, and yes, the beauty we created in spite of all we were confronting.

I began writing about what it's like to live with a rare degenerative disease to share my personal experience, to explore what it means to reimagine your life over and over again. I wanted to bear witness to my family's grief and joy and to take control of the narrative in the one way I knew how.

The more vulnerable I became in my writing, the more others could understand and therefore support my family. But more than that, my vulnerability encouraged people to share their own stories with me too. I realized that though Dalia's disease was rare, living with mystery and pain is something most people experience in one way or another. Sharing our stories binds us together.

Because while each of our stories is unique, there's so much about them that's universal. Whether or not you're personally dealing with an insidious disease, chances are you're trying to create a life of joy and meaning in a world of uncertainty. You're trying to figure out who you are and who you're going to become as the life you once imagined changes shape.

The people you'll read about in this book are so much more than their rare diseases. They're warriors and change-makers, artists and advocates. They're people just like you who want the best for themselves and their families, people who have discovered they're capable of so much more than they once thought.

Together, our stories shed light on the lives of others and on the paths in front of us. May your journey, all our journeys, be lit with hope.

Jessica Fein

Jessica Fein is the author of *Breath Taking: A Memoir of Family, Dreams, and Broken Genes* and host of the *I Don't Know How You Do It* podcast, which features people whose lives seem unimaginable. Her writing has appeared in the *New York Times, Newsweek, Psychology Today, the Boston Globe, HuffPost,* and more. Jessica is a relentless warrior in the memory of her dynamic daughter, whom she lost to rare disease in 2022. Her work encompasses hope and humour, grit and grace—the tools that make up her personal survival kit.

To learn more, visit www.jessicafeinstories.com.

Preface

When I was diagnosed as gene positive for Huntington's disease (a rare disease), I didn't know anyone from the community. I felt like no one in my life understood what I was going through, and I quickly felt isolated, alone, and scared. I started writing about my experiences because I didn't want others to feel the same way, and I thought we could connect through the power of storytelling. Writing and sharing my stories was such a cathartic process that I made it my goal to help others experience the same thing . . . because **every voice deserves to be heard**.

For the past year and half, I have been working on this collaborative book with a group of inspiring and highly dedicated rare disease warriors. They all came to the project with a message they wanted to share. Through one-on-one coaching, I helped them find experiences from their lives that best illustrated their messages. Draft after draft, we worked together to refine their stories.

Not only did they write their stories with such openness and vulnerability, they did so while battling everything life threw at them, including medical setbacks, symptom flare-ups, the passing of loved ones, and the loss of jobs. That's how dedicated they were to this project and to our joint mission of recounting our personal stories to bring awareness to rare diseases, and to be a guiding light for others who are going through similar things.

This book is not just about rare diseases, however. It is about overcoming obstacles, redefining our purpose, accepting the reality of what is, questioning our beliefs, embracing our new identities, and standing up for what is right. Through their stories, these rare disease warriors teach us that **we are so much more than our rare diseases**.

I know you will be inspired by the stories everyone has so bravely shared. Thank you so much for taking the time to read our collaborative anthology. We are so grateful for your compassion, your support, and your understanding.

I look forward to working with more under-represented medical communities over the coming years. There are so many more important stories out there that need to be told. If you have a story you want to share, I would love to hear from you.

Erin Paterson

erin@lemonadecommunity.com
https://lemonadecommunity.com
Instagram: @lemonadepressbooks

One Dream at a Time

A Message from our Premier Sponsor

Jamie's Story

I had just spent the perfect Friday at the office coaching our top real estate agents. I realized I had found my passion, and it brought me so much energy. *What if I could do this every day?* I thought to myself. In my current role I was spending only 20 percent of my week doing what I enjoyed—coaching people and helping them become the best they could be.

A little voice in the back of my head began to have a party. The drums and the beat started softly at first; however, over the next two months it became a full-blown rock concert. I could no longer avoid it. I was at a fork in the road.

I had been in the real estate industry for over thirty-five years, and my role was no longer giving me the joy it once had. I loved the people I worked with, and I still felt connected to them, yet I was different. I didn't fit the mould I had spent years crafting.

I have always invested in my personal development, and that had shifted so much in life that my definition of happiness had changed. I craved deeper relationships, bigger dreams, and a new-found purpose. I walked away from my career in the real estate industry to pursue my dream of helping more people at a deeper level.

As it happened, I began to coach my daughter through a six-month transformational program. It was as if we both started growing along the same path. Slowly the next steps of my journey became clear. This was the start of coming together to create something life changing.

Jacklyn's Story

I was working in the advertising industry, and it was anything but thrilling. Instead it was late nights, early mornings, and low pay with an unhealthy work–life balance. I felt like I was trying to fit into a place I wasn't made for. So many people in the office weren't happy—constantly complaining about the daily duties and office politics, spending countless hours in a career they hated. I knew there had to be something more.

So while I continued working, I invested in Dad's six-month coaching program. The program worked on the stuff that isn't evident in those before-and-after photos you see online. It focused on helping me be the best version of myself, except not just in the physical way. The program helped me identify my core beliefs and change my operating system.

One summer morning, shortly after completing the program, I was battling rush-hour traffic in downtown Toronto on the way to work. I drove into the parking lot and put the car into park. I glanced in the rearview mirror to put on my favourite clear lip gloss, and my hands started to shake. Like clockwork the panic attack hit. My heart started racing, and I could feel sweat building up on my neck. It was as if my body was trying to tell me what my mind was trying to ignore. This job wasn't right for me.

Through my coaching with Dad, I had discovered there was so much more to life than spending all your time in a career that isn't meant for you. I knew I needed to take responsibility to build a life that actually made me happy I quit my job and started to follow a calling that brought a sense of purpose to my life.

That's when my dad, Jamie, and I partnered to launch the Be Do Have Movement.

The Be Do Have Movement: Our Story

We wanted people to know that change is possible, growth is a choice, and their dreams shouldn't be lost. So together we built a business and life-coaching company that transforms lives.

The Be Do Have Movement serves, inspires, and empowers others to have the courage to become the best they can be.

We work with people who believe in something more for themselves too. They know that no matter what hand they are dealt in this world, they will fight to follow their dreams.

That is why we are supporting this book. We believe in the power of coming together to support other people who are courageously using their voices for change. Whether it's offering hope to someone else or reassurance that they aren't alone, our goal is to make an individual impact that creates a ripple effect of positive change, one person and one dream at a time.

Chapter 1: The Birth of a Dragon Mom

By Laura Will

I hunched over Alden, our four-month-old son, for another diaper change. It was quiet, except for a soft crinkle as my fingertips reached into the bag of baby wipes. My mind was elsewhere. Alden did not coo or babble. His eyes were fixed on the dramatic striped pattern of the window next to us, where daylight snuck into his nursery through the wooden slats of the blinds. As I guided his tiny toes back into a light-yellow onesie, I felt a muscle twitching in his right ankle; my angsty stomach churned once again. For weeks something had seemed not quite right with Alden's movements. I had taken him into his pediatrician's office earlier that day. She had said Alden was fine, but I remained apprehensive.

I took my phone out and searched for videos on how to evaluate a newborn for signs of cerebral palsy, which was the diagnosis that kept coming, unbidden, into my mind. Part mom and part clinician, I propped the phone on the end of the changing table and completed a homespun neurological exam. I felt queasy. He had performed very poorly. Picking Alden up after this derailed diaper change, I wondered if my postpartum fatigue was tipping me into a nightmarish delusion.

Over the next couple of days, whenever I voiced my concerns about my internet-guided neurological findings, my husband would look at me, not Alden, with concern. We both knew I was struggling to develop a loving connection with our son. Despite my medical training as an adult-geriatric nurse practitioner, my husband trusted that the pediatrician knew more about infant development than his sleep-deprived and stress-prone wife; and so I doubted my evaluation and myself.

A week later, I again witnessed repetitive spastic movements, but this time I managed to catch them on video with my phone. It was Memorial Day weekend, so I called the pediatrician on-call service. Summoning my most authoritative clinical language and swagger, I requested to be connected to a pediatric neurologist and explained my concerns again. The resident asked that I text him the video; it was quickly reviewed, and I was told to bring Alden into the emergency room. My heart fluttered with a combination of anxiety and relief that finally someone was taking my concerns seriously. While my husband, Dave, clipped Alden's tiny frame into his infant car seat by the front door, I hurried to our bedroom and stuffed my phone charger and some extra clothes for both Alden and me into the backpack we used as a diaper bag. It was 2020 and COVID numbers were spiking in the Boston area, so only one adult was allowed to accompany each child at the hospital. Dave held the front door open as I headed out to the car with the backpack in one hand and car seat in the other.

Alden was admitted. Forty-eight hours later the attending pediatric neurologist, whom I had watched evaluate our son with a rotating cast of students and specialists over the last two days, walked into Alden's hospital room wearing a grim look on her face. A young resident trailed in afterwards, placing a miniature can of ginger ale and a packet of saltine crackers next to me and offering to hold Alden while we talked. This was not going to be good news. The sharp smell of hand sanitizer hung in the air between us. The attending physician sat down next to me and suggested we get my husband on speaker phone. She proceeded to explain that, according to the initial MRI report, our son had been born with a rare brain malformation called polymicrogyria. She avoided getting into many details, suggesting instead that I take Alden home. She would call us later so Dave and I could be together as we processed the news.

When Alden and I got home, Dave repeated something the neurologist had said, that "this diagnosis would not change his personality." I was too distraught to begin to understand what she had meant by that. Our son was a taciturn and spastic infant. His personality was a complete mystery. Instead, the word *malformation* played on repeat in my mind, with its Latin origin of *mal-* signifying bad, ill, wrong. Language matters, and medicine had just labelled our child a deformity.

Before the neurologist called that evening to give us a more in-depth report of the MRI findings, I skimmed the most recent research articles I could find on polymicrogyria. Polymicrogyria describes a pattern of brain folds in the outermost cerebral cortex of the brain that are too small and too frequent, resulting in less functional brain matter and increased risk of seizure activity. While there are treatment options for seizure control and therapies to support motor and speech development, there is no hope of curing the underlying cause. I learned that there is a large spectrum in terms of brain area that may be affected. Some people live with polymicrogyria on a small portion of their cerebral cortex and are seemingly completely unaffected, only learning of it as an incidental finding. That being said, polymicrogyria most often presents in the areas of the brain that control speech production, resulting in limited verbal skills. But in severe cases, it is everywhere—affecting both sides of the brain and all the lobes, resulting in profound physical and cognitive disability. I read through case studies and posts from parents on Facebook groups, calculating degrees of disability, inappropriately placing them on a mental hierarchy as I waited for my phone to ring.

As the sun set that evening, I sat nursing our baby boy, my fingertips gently tapping the fuzzy hair on his head. He felt familiar in my arms but foreign to my mind, adrift in uncertainty and fear. I recalled images and facts from graduate school lectures that focused on disability rights: the national transition away from soulless institutions that housed individuals with deformity and intellectual disability; laws promoting the structural changes to public transportation and buildings; and the push for integration and representation in schools, sports, and work. I am sure I studied my lecture notes with the desire to understand, but it had all seemed distant. Now my parental journey was taking a dramatic turn, and I struggled to envision the path ahead with this little boy in my arms. Unprocessed ableist beliefs were obscuring the value of his life and the adapted adventures ahead for both of us. Despite my education and empathy, I had subtly internalized societal prejudices of disability as a sad or diminished aberration of the "normal" human experience.

I swaddled his tiny body, snuggly securing the soft blanket around his legs and arms. My hands held his innocence as my frazzled mind sifted through images of disabled people, marginalized by a society not designed for inclusion or primed for understanding. I could not yet envision what a joyful, successful future for our child and our family would entail. I had not yet learned how to engineer my dreams for our family to make them accessible. I did not yet know that within the realms of non-verbal communication, an expansive connection beyond words blossoms beautifully. I had not met the physical therapists, schoolteachers, and empathetic strangers that would guide me as I peeled away limiting assumptions to truly embrace the value of Alden's life. I still had to learn that disability rights are, quite simply, human rights.

My phone rang, lighting up with "NO CALLER ID." I jumped to answer it, crying out to Dave, "It's the neurologist," in a constricted, slightly breathless voice. We settled in next to each other on the edge of our bed, with the phone held on an open palm between us, as we learned that Alden's brain was severely affected. The malformation was practically everywhere. I peppered the neurologist with questions—trying to understand, trying to predict, trying to prepare. Meanwhile, Dave quietly absorbed what he could. Alden would live with moderate to severe physical and cognitive disability, with a shortened life expectancy, at high risk for seizures that would become difficult to control. This was not fixable.

We hung up the phone, and I imagine we held each other. I cannot remember what we said, but I know it was impossible to hold each other's grief in addition to the weight of our own. I peered into Alden's bassinet beside our bed and felt nauseous. We climbed into bed for the night. I turned to lay my head on Dave's chest. Always an impeccable sleeper, he nodded off. Hours later I was still awake, my cheeks soggy with tears and snot. My head pounded, pinned at the excruciating intersection of fear and grief. Expectations about the child Alden was supposed to be, expectations I had not even realized I had, came unbidden into my mind; and each one was met with a staggering sense of loss. While acutely painful, this was part of the process: I was deeply grieving the loss of the child I had expected.

I sobbed with the thought that Alden would never marry, never father a child. The ache of this realization surprised me; and yet I wondered if some ancient instinct had known he was, in terms of evolutionary biology, a "non-viable offspring." I had sensed a poor attachment to Alden from the time I started to notice something seemed maladaptive—his trouble nursing, poor eye contact, strange motor patterns. I had been dutifully executing the tasks of motherhood in a numbly detached manner for weeks. Perhaps this detachment was informed by a subconscious knowing, a protective instinct. The truth of the matter is that not long ago or in a different part of the world today, without gastronomy tubes and seizure medications, Alden would have died before his second birthday. With the medical interventions and support we can provide him, he may live well into early adulthood.

As we started to share the news that Alden's life would be dramatically different, finding the wording that felt right was a process of trial and error. In return, many reactions from friends and family in the first couple of weeks were steeped in poorly informed narratives and assumptions about disability. One family member referenced the latest gene-editing research, suggesting that science could rebuild our boy's brain. Another referred to him as a "ball and chain" that would limit our family life, asking if there was perhaps a facility where we could take him—and leave him, permanently. This particular comment was from someone who's perspective I trusted, and I found myself spinning. I researched whether there was such a thing as a place to house Alden, and then was repulsed with myself for having done so. We also had individuals in our support network with intolerably positive attitudes or near complete denial. It was exhausting and sometimes futile, but I found myself counterbalancing the positivity and denial, verbalizing hard truths again and again. We were all processing this in our own ways, and we all had a lot to learn. More often than not, the language and attitudes of others were emotionally destabilizing for me. Even seemingly innocent questions could trigger deep grief, frustration, or fear.

As a means of personal survival, I invested heavily in self-care in those early months post-diagnosis, connecting with a grief counsellor and starting a daily dose of an antidepressant medication. I set boundaries with family who were not able to be supportive in the ways I needed at that time, and I prohibited any questions about anything more than six months in the future. I took the first steps towards meeting Alden's needs as a child living with disability and complex medical needs, such as initiating early intervention programming, setting up a swallow study, and proactively connecting with an epileptologist to have a plan of care in place prior to his seizure activity onset. It was clear that this version of motherhood was going to take a lot of time, coordination, energy, and devotion.

There were countless forms to be filled out. Each one required that I regurgitate his diagnosis details and growing list of missed developmental milestones. Each one required I list my name and relationship to the patient: mother. But the word *mother* never seemed to fill the line on the page. The word *mother* did not quite capture my relationship to this child. The word felt too commonplace for the vast and weighty responsibility of mothering Alden.

On a late summer afternoon, I saw myself in my bedroom mirror. I paused, turning towards my reflection, holding Alden's tiny body against my chest. It had been three months since receiving his diagnosis, and he had missed all his six-month developmental milestones. I looked tired. I was tired. There was so much to manage in terms of appointments and emotions; and it seemed like Alden's brain was delayed, among other things, in learning how to sleep through the night. I asked myself, "Mother?" No, the word *mother* would not suffice. It needed an additive or qualifier. "Mother of a child with disabilities and medical complexity?" Too wordy. "Special needs mom?" It certainly did not feel *special*, and I had learned this language was an aging relic of the Americans with Disabilities Act. And so, with a deep exhale, I thought, *Dragon mom.*

I had recently read an opinion article by Emily Rapp, a mother of a child with a fatal neurodegenerative disease. In the article, she notes that traditional parenting models and mindsets are based on the assumption that we will launch our children into a future beyond us, where they will achieve some version of success as defined by societal standards. I immediately identified with Rapp as she explained our parental goals as "simple and terrible: to help our children live with minimal discomfort and maximum dignity." She goes on to explain: "This requires a new ferocity, a new way of thinking, a new animal. We are dragon parents: fierce and loyal and loving as hell."[1] Slowly inhaling the sweet baby smell, I squeezed Alden more tightly to my chest and envisioned wings unfurling behind me, and a tail's smooth underside and spiked dorsal ridge extending beyond the frame of the mirror.

A dragon mom was born.

The dragon mom identity has become a wonderful tool. Prior to appointments or social outings that I know will be particularly challenging or triggering, I envision zipping into my dragon suit, my invisible armour, both strong and protective. It is tailored to help me face a world not designed with my child's needs in mind and the people

1 Emily Rapp, "Notes from a Dragon Mom," *New York Times* (October 15, 2011). www.nytimes.com/2011/10/16/opinion/sunday/notes-from-a-dragon-mom.html

in that world who pity Alden or lack empathy due to their limiting beliefs or lack of exposure. Sometimes, when reflecting on the day with my husband, I note, "I needed my dragon suit today." And he knows that whatever I have gone through—perhaps advocating for a more sophisticated assistive speech device or emotionally navigating my way through one of his neurotypical peer's birthday parties—required more than the average mother.

And yet, with my human heart, I am still vulnerable. I continue to experience the natural and often unexpected waves of grief that are inherent to dragon motherhood, such as when I went searching for a developmentally appropriate birthday gift for Alden's second birthday. Standing in the toy store, surrounded by cheerful images of neurotypical, able-bodied children on the packaging of toys, I scanned the aisle with increasing desperation, hoping for a toy that Alden's uncoordinated body could play with and enjoy. My heart began to ache. Out of the corner of my eye, the infant section, with its little stuffed animals, simple board books, and oversized-button toys, taunted me. Those toys were perhaps still most appropriate for my child, but I refused to look at them and instead fled the store. Regaining composure in the parking lot, I realized that acceptance is not a final destination. I had accepted having a disabled infant—and all that entailed. But at this next birthday, I began the work of accepting all over again, this time with a toddler who could not—and would not—toddle.

Each milestone missed became a new practice in acceptance, some easier than others. With each act of letting go of expectations came a deepening connection to the essence of who Alden is: his joy, his innate personhood, the spark that shines within. Despite the fact that at three years old, Alden had still not learned to sit up independently, sip through a straw, or begin to babble, it became clear that the boundaries and barriers I placed on his life, and mine as his mother, were based on what I believed this might look like and feel like.

While the caregiving and coordination are demanding, Alden has added extraordinary texture to our family life, connecting us with people, ideas, and experiences we would have never known without him. We have been supported and changed by other dragon parents, caring clinicians, and adaptive athletes. As much as possible, my husband and I jettisoned the mentality of "milestones" and replaced it with a family culture that celebrates "Aldenstones," a unique unit of measurement that acknowledges the whole person: the physical, emotional, humorous, and curious being that Alden continues to reveal to us. For me, it has been an intentional evolution beyond primal instincts and ableist ideas. It has become a radical and regular practice of empathy and presence. We love Alden here and now, for how he is and who he is today, without categorization or conditions. This is an extraordinary way to love anyone.

We celebrated his fourth birthday this year. Surrounded by friends and family, he sat smiling at our dining room table in an activity chair that offers him the support his body needs. Lacking breath control, he used a small hand-held fan to blow out his birthday candles. Unable to chew and swallow solid food safely, he had a plate piled high with frosting only. It looks different; but it sure is sweet.

Laura is raising a child born with polymicrogyria.

Bilateral generalized **polymicrogyria** is a rare neurological disorder that affects the cerebral cortex (the outer surface of the brain). This is the most widespread form of polymicrogyria and typically affects the entire surface of the brain. Signs and symptoms include severe intellectual disability, problems with movement, and seizures that are difficult or impossible to treat. While the exact cause of bilateral generalized polymicrogyria is not fully understood, it is thought to be due to improper brain development during embryonic growth. Most cases appear to follow an autosomal recessive pattern of inheritance. Treatment is based on the signs and symptoms present in each person.

https://rarediseases.org/mondo-disease/bilateral-generalized-polymicrogyria/

Source: NORD

Laura Will lives in Concord, Massachusetts, with her husband Dave, her three children, and her son's service dog, Buoy. Laura earned a master's degree in nursing from Columbia University in 2014. Her middle child, Alden, was born with a rare brain malformation in 2020. She now works at Know Rare, helping educate and uplift the rare disease patient community and support rare disease clinical research. Laura also runs a grant-funded virtual support group for parents of medically complex children through Cape Cod Children's Place. Laura and Dave are dedicated supporters of Mass General for Children and Courageous Parents Network, contributing regularly to their missions of improving health and well-being for children with complex illnesses and their families. Follow her story @ adragonmomswords or www.adragonmomswords.com.

Chapter 2: The Perfect Mother

By Courtney Wells

As soon as I stood up, a violent dizziness slammed into me, clobbering me like a thousand-pound wrecking ball. I was so sick that when I was standing, I needed to keep taking breaks and resting my head on whatever horizontal surfaces were available. Although I felt pretty rotten, I wasn't the least bit surprised, considering my house was inhabited by three walking elementary-aged Petri dishes. I was a vibrant, busy, sociable mother of three children under age ten. It was rare when at least one of us wasn't sick with something. You might read this litany of symptoms and think, *Good grief, woman! Why weren't you in bed?!* The answer is simple. It was five days until Halloween! My favourite holiday of the year.

I had too much to do to be sick, and as an incredibly stubborn person, I was determined to manifest the perfect holiday for my kids. There was no room on my busy agenda for illness. I had costumes to complete, and equally importantly, I had seventy-five cupcakes for three separate classrooms to finish. As was my holiday routine, I was making and decorating treats—always from scratch! I was well known for making thematic baking contributions to any special occasion, and teachers often praised me for being so crafty and talented. Most importantly, my kids were so proud of the awesome baking that *their* mom could do, and no way would I let them down.

This particular Halloween, I had undertaken graveyard dirt cupcakes. They had toxic-waste-green wrappers, which enveloped chocolate cupcakes, heaped with an Oreo cookie buttercream. Each cupcake was then adorned with a paper tombstone affixed to a toothpick, tiny candy bones, and spider-shaped sprinkles. I remember thinking how important it was that each of the cupcakes had the exact same number of decorations.

Halloween day came. I had carefully packaged cupcakes to deliver and excited kids to get costumed at lunch-hour recess. Both girls insisted that I help with their respective costumes and makeup, vying loudly as to whom I would dress first. My son, on the other hand, was already quite conscious of how "uncool" it was to have your *mom* dress you. Nothing was going to get between him and those classroom cupcakes though; the cacophony of their high voices was deafening.

The noise only added to the overall feeling of sick I was still experiencing. The dizziness and nausea were leg irons, hobbling me as I navigated the crowded halls of the elementary school. It took every ounce of my will to put one foot solidly in front of the other, but I was accustomed to being uncomfortable and stubbornly pushing forward.

I had been born a klutz. Throughout my childhood and adolescence and into adulthood, I was always nursing a new injury, or dealing with the lingering consequences of an old one. I had suffered from migraines increasing in intensity, frequency, and duration since my teens. I'd also struggled with a myriad of medical maladies and complications, along with navigating rare side effects and adverse reactions from prescription medications. My first pregnancy, for example, saw me frighteningly diagnosed with a complete placenta previa at eighteen weeks gestation. I complied with all prescribed precautions and still developed a scary bleed, and I lost a significant amount of blood upon my son's birth. Needless to say, if I survived that, I was certain I could manage some nausea and dizziness. To me, my children's Halloween plans were written in stone, but my body did not agree with my stubborn brain's weighty goals.

The school hallways appeared to lengthen with every step I took, making the distance to the exit stretch farther and farther away. The goblins, witches, and zombies running by became a kaleidoscope of changing colours. This only worsened my dizziness, which had become so violent I felt like I was spinning uncontrollably in circles. In that rotating haze of costumes, I began to feel dissociated from my environment. I felt trapped within a maelstrom and I was desperate to escape. At that moment, I knew I needed to seek medical attention. I staggered down the hallway, holding onto the walls for balance, to the main exit.

I left the school and headed straight to the doctor's office. I must have looked as bad as I felt because, despite the fact it was lunch hour, I saw my family doctor immediately. I remember how puzzled my doctor looked while assessing my vital signs. I was lying down on the exam table because otherwise I would have fallen. My vital signs were completely normal, but my ashen complexion, sweat-soaked clothing, and desperate hold on the bed must have belied their perfection. While initially my doctor posited that I probably just had vertigo or a viral ear infection, his demeanour changed in an instant when I stood up. I was immediately thrown back into a tiny rowboat, being tossed around by violent, white-capped waters. My doctor jumped quickly to support me and to take standing vitals. My pulse was now an alarming 200 beats per minute (bpm), and my blood pressure was registering around 60/40. For reference, the normal range for a person my age and sex is 60 to 80 bpm for heart rate and 120/80 for blood pressure. Needless to say, my doctor was beginning to have concerns.

I was ordered up to the town's hospital. It's all such a blur I don't even remember how I got there. There were multiple tests; words and phrases like *for observation, admit, normal 12-lead* swirled around. The lights were too bright, and it felt like I was randomly being wheeled from room to room; the painful stiffness of the gurney and the institutional yellow of the walls were the only constants.

Suddenly, a loud, rapid double bang snapped me out of the confusing funhouse. Ambulance doors had slammed in front of me. I had been plunged into the darkness of the patient compartment. I stared out of the small rear windows into the inky blackness outside, picturing a little box of popcorn trick-or-treating without her mama for the first time in her life. I was bitterly disappointed that I wasn't out there in the jack-o'-lantern–illuminated night. My heart clenched at the thought of my kids running with wild abandon from house to house without me. I finally started to feel settled when I was admitted to a room, but then two paramedics walked through the door rolling a stretcher and shockingly informed me that I was being transferred to another hospital.

While my kids were sorting their candy, I arrived at the aging edifice of a Saskatchewan hospital. The setting could not have been imagined better by Stephen King himself. The hospital sat in a low-income, high-crime neighbourhood with condemned and boarded-up buildings. I was surrounded by a cacophony of scary and unfamiliar sounds: voices raised in anger, alarms blaring, and radios squawking incoherently. I felt vulnerable as I watched security personnel on high alert and RCMP officers coming and going. Paramedics lined the halls, waiting with their patients, the hallways crowded like freeways clogged with rush-hour traffic jams. On the best possible day, this hospital has a frightening emergency department. Late on Halloween night, it's a nightmare-scape.

The paramedics who had given me a measure of comfort, reassurance, and care rolled me into that hellmouth of a hospital and left. I remember trying to catch their attention, to ask them when they'd be back to take me home. But the doors whooshed shut behind them and I knew I was on my own. I felt vulnerable, abandoned, and utterly alone in an unfamiliar, dirty, and loud place two and a half hours away from my home and my babies.

The next week consisted of a rotating cast of nurses and doctors and a never-ending litany of tests. On that first terrible night, I was instructed to essentially "stay in bed and do nothing without assistance," but on the first full day, those orders became ironclad rules when I blacked out after being aided to stand upright for vitals to be taken. I became 100 percent reliant on the hospital staff for every need that required leaving my bed, and with that the last ashes of my autonomy were firmly swept away.

The remnants of my dignity followed shortly after. I was wheeled to the bathroom; I was wheeled into and out of the showers. Oftentimes, they would kill two birds with one stone and put me on a special shower/toilet seat. It was utterly humiliating but economical in terms of movement and body stress. I would be dressed in a simple hospital gown and transferred to a large plastic wheelchair with a hole in the seat. This made it easy for whatever care aide was working that day to roll me over the toilet, at which time I would relieve myself. Next I was rolled into a shower room, where my gown was removed. It honestly felt like I was a car at a self-serve wash. I would be sprayed down, after which I was given the option to soap myself; they would rinse me off, including my "undercarriage."

I was no longer allowed to walk at all. I was told that my heart was working at 95 percent intensity, which was dangerously high. Yet every medical test came back negative. I was assigned to an internal medicine doctor, who told me outright that my presentation puzzled her and that she was struggling to find a diagnosis.

I was desperate for answers and yearning to get home to my family. My husband and children were only able to visit once during that week. I was left with nothing but time, so I turned inward and began researching my symptoms. I spent hours daily, hunched over my phone, my face illuminated by its tiny screen as I typed madly. I spent my research time reading peer-reviewed articles, one after another, and I came to only one conclusion—postural orthostatic tachycardia syndrome, a common autonomic nervous system disorder. Symptoms of POTS include an excessively fast heart rate and light-headedness upon standing. I shyly presented my findings to a nurse with whom I had bonded over our shared love of true crime podcasts. To my amazement, she had been doing research of her own and had reached the same conclusion. She promised she would discuss it with the doctor.

Ultimately, I was diagnosed with POTS. The doctor explained it was a diagnosis of exclusion, which means it's what's left over after every other condition has been eliminated. The mystery was solved! And then the doctor immediately lost interest in me. I remember her saying, "I would love to keep you as a patient because you're compliant and a nice person, but the management for this condition can be done at home. You'll need to drink more water and increase your sodium intake."

I remember feeling flabbergasted. Nothing had changed! My heart was still working at 95 percent intensity, and I would still black out if I stood up. I was prescribed midodrine, with a stern warning that it could cause postural hypertension (high blood pressure when lying down). The initial feelings of victory and success that came with naming this terrifying, mysterious thing turned sour and depressing. My rubric for success was the ability to return home immediately and still be the identical mom who had left. But there was to be only failure. The woman who returned home wasn't the one who had left. She had ceased to exist.

With the support of my family physician, I was transferred back to the small health centre where this odyssey had begun. Despite what the diagnosing physician had said, "mystery solved" never meant I could go home. My family physician had to take on the heavy burden of learning to manage my dangerous symptoms of high pulse rate, low blood pressure, and repeated fainting on standing. I still naively thought I'd be home before mid-November, which was wishful thinking at its finest. No one could find the appropriate combination of drugs and lifestyle modifications that would manage my dangerous symptoms.

The dreaded shower chair remained a routine part of my life, and I was still bereft of my dignity. The most painful memory I associate with that aspect of my stay was when a lovely care aide suddenly exclaimed while shampooing my hair, "Oh my God, Courtney, your hair is just falling out!" She held soapy hands up in front of my face, and they were encased in my hair. I had no physical autonomy to speak of, my self-confidence was taking a brutal beating, and I was desperately lonely for my husband and children, as they were for me. By the beginning of December, I had started to receive hysterical calls nightly from my children. They were terrified that I'd miss Christmas. Even though they visited every day around suppertime, it just wasn't enough. I was a ghost.

I knew, without a doubt, that I had to make it home for Christmas. Preparing for the holiday itself was easy: I bought all of the Christmas gifts online. But I still had to conquer the seemingly insurmountable battle of successfully managing my POTS and overcoming the consequences of my enforced inactivity. Research was one way I felt like I could fight the war.

I fell back to my previous pattern of long nights hunched over my cell phone, combing through research papers and scientific articles. I couldn't reconcile how I was brought so low by POTS, just out of the blue. As my research progressed, I recognized a pattern. Dysautonomia (which POTS is a form of) is a common feature of very few other conditions, the most common being Ehlers-Danlos syndrome (EDS). I learned there are thirteen types of EDS; all but one are diagnosed genetically. That single one is instead diagnosed clinically with a series of questions organized into the Beighton scale. Excitedly, I had my husband print information from The Ehlers-Danlos Society, which included instructions on administering the Beighton scale. I immediately determined that I scored 9 out of 9, and it felt vitally important to pass my findings on to the doctor. He brushed my research aside. When I tried to give him the physical printouts, he declined to look at them. He argued that complicating an already complex situation with a potentially unrelated diagnosis was a distraction. I immediately dropped the topic, although I was disappointed by his outright dismissal of something I felt was relevant to the situation as a whole. Ultimately, confrontation with my doctor didn't feel like the way to accomplish my goal to get home.

In the end, the missing piece of the POTS management puzzle wasn't found because of my stubborn determination to conduct my own research. Instead, an old and familiar medical complication revealed the solution. I suffered an adverse reaction to the medication prescribed by the internist at the hospital where I spent my first week. As she had cautioned weeks before, postural hypertension reared its ugly head. One early December night, seemingly out of nowhere, I was overcome with a hair-raising feeling of dread. My heart went haywire. It was one of the most terrifying events of my entire life. The nurse on shift had to run and grab a crash cart. I remember her saying I might need to be transferred back to that other hospital.

One singular thought pierced the terror: "I can't ruin Christmas!"

The scariest night of my life was a blessing in disguise. I was extremely lucky that the beta blocker medication my quick-thinking doctor used to control my postural hypertension and stop the crisis also managed the tachycardia side of POTS. There was finally some light shining dimly in the darkness.

The only step between me and beautiful illumination was regaining the ability to walk independently. I had largely been confined to bed for almost a month and a half. I had lost muscle mass, muscle strength, stamina, and coordination. I had largely lost my ability to walk. It took me nearly two weeks to learn how to walk again, and then only supported by a rollator walker.

I made it home in time for Christmas! Joyfully it was the least stressful Christmas I'd had in years. Nothing else mattered on that beautiful holiday, except that I was with my husband and kids. I snuggled my kids as much as I possibly could and marvelled at the privilege of just being with them.

Sadly, my joy and triumph could not resurrect the part of me who died in that terrifying emergency department on Halloween night. The Courtney of before is gone forever. Physically, I lost my autonomy. I remain unstable on my feet. I use a variety of mobility devices (cane, crutches, rollator walker, Alinker walking bike, and wheelchair) to facilitate my movement through the world. My body is unpredictable. One day I can have almost normal movement, and the next I need a walker. Over the intervening years, I've tried to rebuild myself in many ways but never successfully. I also had my dignity stripped away. As a result, my self-confidence and self-esteem suffered dramatically. I have never regained the feeling that my body belongs wholly to me. I also struggle tremendously with my sense of self-worth, as my dysautonomia has permanently disabled me. I tire extremely quickly; exhaustion often leads to illness, which increases my risk of developing other complications. Ultimately, the most devastating loss I've suffered is the sociable person I used to be. I had friend groups, in addition to close long-term friendships spanning decades, but people in my life began to drift away, which is deeply isolating and depressing.

In June 2020, a rheumatologist spontaneously (he did not know of my prior research) diagnosed me with hypermobility EDS, or hEDS. At the time of the diagnosis, he went on to explain that I had scored highly on the Beighton scale, and my history (childhood injuries, klutziness, joint injuries that never fully healed) combined with my high score indicated that I likely had hEDS or EDS type III. Strangely, my initial diagnosis brought with it a sense of peace. It was such a relief to know that my klutziness was not at all something I had control over! My crippling headaches finally had explanation; even my predilection for enduring uncommon complications like placenta previa now has a probable reason.

Today, most of my major joints are demonstrating crepitus (bone grinding against bone), even though I'm only in my early forties. Injuries I sustained at a young age are effectively crippling me. My right knee is destroyed and already requires a replacement. My back has been described by my diagnosing rheumatologist as a ticking time bomb; he predicts that I will be wheelchair dependent by the time I'm fifty. I also live with a tremendous amount of ongoing pain. A chronic pain specialist who assessed me a month ago said that EDS is one of the major culprits responsible for severe chronic pain.

I refuse, however, to let what's left of my life be about misery and pain. Beauty has also blossomed over the last four years. My children have grown into tweens and teens. Gone are the tiny hands and chubby faces I so missed during my time away. In their stead are acne, lengthening limbs, and loudly argued opinions. After all the adversity I've faced, my most stubborn battle by far has been to stay the best mom possible for my kids. My disability and loss of autonomy have taught me that being a good mom isn't showing the world just how fantastic you are. In a parenting generation that's become obsessed with presenting an Instagram-perfect life defined by flawless mothers, over-the-top holiday parties, and marvellous home-baked confections, being a good mom is based on what other people can see. I realize in retrospect that my early parenting years were spent entirely too conscious of what other people thought. I was obsessed with perfection. I was so busy running around doing everything society expected of the perfect mom that I lost sight of what was most important to my kids.

My hospitalization taught me that what my kids value most is spending time together. My illness has given me the time and space to build a highly individualized relationship with each of my kids, to get to know them as people. I parent with far more empathy, time, and patience, and I sincerely feel I've become a better mom as a result. The fact that I need to stay close to home means I'm almost always available for a cuddle or a heart-to-heart talk. I won't lie and say that I don't worry every day about what effect this adversity will have on them going forward. However, I hope they'll always remember how hard their mom fought to make her way back to them and continues to fight to stay.

Courtney is living with Ehlers-Danlos syndrome type III.

Ehlers-Danlos syndrome (EDS) is a group of related disorders caused by different genetic defects in collagen, one of the major structural components of the body. Patients with EDS often have skin that can be described as "loose." This skin characteristic predisposes patients to problems with wound healing. Patients will often note that they develop "paper-thin" scars. Patients also have excessively flexible, loose joints. These hypermobile joints can be easily and frequently dislocated. Finally, fragile blood vessels leave patients experiencing easy bruising, even an increased tendency to serious episodes of bleeding.

https://rarediseases.org/rare-diseases/ehlers-danlos-syndrome/
Source: NORD

Courtney Wells is an advocate for people living with invisible illness and disability. She talks about her lived experience on the Apple podcast *I Am Not My Pain*, and she was interviewed by CBC Radio in Saskatchewan about an appalling ER visit while searching for answers about her own rare disease. She hails from Edmonton, Alberta, and currently lives in both Senlac and Unity, Saskatchewan, splitting her time between farm and small-town life with her husband, three children, five cats, two dogs, and a flock of evolved egg-laying velociraptors. In her spare time, Courtney rehabilitates "hard cases" for her local cat rescue, rescues plants in need for her home jungle, and collects bones, taxidermy, and wet specimens. Consequently, she dreams of the perfect curio display combined with a utopian plant cabinet. She also believes in dragons. Courtney can be found on Facebook at www.facebook.com/courtney.a.wells and Instagram @quirkyowl.

Chapter 3: We Are All Advocates

By Daniel DeFabio director of community engagement at Global Genes, our charity partner

When my son, Lucas, was diagnosed at just over twelve months old, with the ultra-rare genetic disease Menkes syndrome, our world spun into something we could never have anticipated. It took a few years for my wife and I to get beyond fear and preoccupation with the daily urgent care needs of our son and begin to find some new understanding of the life ahead for all three of us. An understanding that set aside so many assumptions and expectations of what our life *should* be like. We needed to allow ourselves to find the joys in this new life despite the dire prognosis for our only child. Boys with Menkes syndrome are estimated to live three to ten years. Most will not walk or talk or be able to eat, sit, or perform controlled movement without assistance. And yet we discovered our beautiful boy was filled with laughs, grins, and mischief, his sparkling, crystal blue eyes daring anyone around him not to smile.

The first thing we did to salve the anguish of this new diagnosis was drive an hour east with Lucas to the modern art museum Mass MoCA. We were seeking distraction but also trying to prove we could still function in basic ways and test whether an appreciation of beauty and art could break through our foreboding gloom. The cavernous warehouse spaces turned into galleries, and the larger-than-life sculptures lent a sense of scale vast enough that it might make our concerns seem smaller. More importantly, it turned out Lucas loved it there. I can still see his face as he took in a simple mobile made from repurposed shiny candy wrappers dangling and twisting before his thirteen-month-old eyes. Wonder gushed from his grin, which stretched from one ice blue eye to the other. Snuggled into a chest pack carrier, he was nearly the height of the artwork. It was clear he couldn't stretch his eyes open wide enough to take in as much of this amazing new sight as he wished.

After we left that exhibit behind, Lucas was enthralled by an even simpler marvel. It was not another art installation but oddly it was also recycling related. I was ready to discard a coffee cup in a low bin for recycling. I saw Lucas watching me and decided to hold the cup six feet above the bin before letting it drop. Lucas tracked all of this and found the disappearance of the cup to be a crack-up delight. He laughed like he was in on the joke. As if he were the magician who rigged up this vanishing act. I found another cup and repeated the trick. Even more delight and giggles.

Of course this was likely just the persistence of the object permanence development stage a baby goes through. It never entered my mind to question whether this was happening for Lucas on schedule or with a delay in his development. In that moment it didn't matter. The only thing that mattered was the joy—the joy he felt and reflected back out to the world with a multiplier effect.

In the coming months, this would be my North Star to guide us through difficult medical care decisions: Are we allowing for more joy in, for, and from Lucas?

Menkes syndrome is rare among the rare, as it is one of the few rare diseases with a known treatment. A simple daily injection can mean a much longer life with closer to typical health. Boys (Menkes is almost always found in boys) who receive the shots in time walk, talk, eat, play sports and music, and live into their twenties or thirties.

But note I said if they receive the shots *in time*.

This therapy of copper histidinate injections is effective only if begun in the first ten days of life. In my son's case, he did get those shots through a clinical trial but not within that critical window of time. Despite spending the first ten days of his life in a NICU where he was seen by specialists, including neurology, none of Lucas's doctors were familiar enough with Menkes syndrome to suspect it and order the genetic test for it. He had been born with an unexplained fracture to the occipital area of his skull. Doctor after doctor was baffled. There were urgent efforts to discover if he had any brain bleeds or brain damage. When those tests showed all clear and with some recovery time, after ten days we were discharged.

To be fair to those doctors, most symptoms of Menkes syndrome may not present until four to nine months of age. One of the few indications at birth is brittle, twisted hair. This is why Menkes has the useful nickname "kinky hair syndrome." I hate to play the "if only" game, but if only one of our doctors during those ten days had heard of Menkes syndrome before and knew a telltale sign was kinky hair, Lucas could have lived a much healthier and longer life. This is why newborn sequencing is so important for so many rare diseases, Menkes in particular.

I can still vividly recall the crushing dread that struck me each of those early days. Weekdays I'd drop Lucas off in the morning at my mom's house. She generously and adoringly provided his day care for the first couple of years. My drive back home in solitude was one of the rare moments of my day for quiet reflection. That was when the urgent panic of the needs in the now gave space for the looming dread of what was to come.

My route and the time of day typically put me behind a school bus as it made its several stops picking up young students. Red lights flashed warnings at me. The bus's octagon sign told me to stop. A dark cloud of exhaust obscured my view ahead. This was an obstacle I could not pass or go around. Stuck behind the bulk of the bus, I had even less busy-ness to distract me, not even the simple activity of driving. In this forced stillness, my heart would sink watching those kids as I thought, *My boy will never climb onto a school bus with his friends. Will he even have friends?* Lucas was less than two years old, so school for him was a few years off. But the time and distance 'til then felt like an uncrossable road. It seemed impossible to imagine him as one of those kids going to class each day.

It was one of my lowest moments of the day, and it recurred nearly five days a week until he reached pre-school age. I didn't know the language for it then, but this was a time of grief. Grieving my expectations, the expectations of a "normal" childhood. Of course any parent would expect their child to someday get on a bus, go to school, make friends, graduate . . . and then . . . and then . . . But there probably would not be an "and then" for Lucas. In fact, he might not experience any of those things.

But when Lucas was five, he was approved to go to a special-needs kindergarten class. I was delighted to see some of those dreads of mine proved wrong. A different sort of bus would pull up to our driveway each morning. The shorter kind of bus. Its rear door opened, and the whine of the slowly lowered lift meant Lucas could be rolled on board in his wheelchair. One of my very favourite memories is the day his arrival was greeted by another student on the bus with a very excited yell of "Lukey is here! And he brought popcorn!" He had not brought popcorn, but the enthusiasm, even the simple recognition of my boy as a welcome part of a group of other students, melted my heart. Lucas did get to board a school bus; he did make friends. Not in the ways I had expected. Not in the ways I watched those other kids a few years before as I waited behind their bigger bus. This was my education: that things would certainly be different, but not all of the differences were bad or less than—they just differed from my expected ideals. Amid all the new unexpected pains there would also be new unexpected joys. Slowly learning this may have been what freed my mind to allow me to live our life and not just get through our life.

As we got a better grasp on managing his day-to-day routine—catheters every three hours, tube feeds twice a day plus overnight, three to six meds three times a day, diapering (long past the typical age, in fact for his entire life), therapies, lifting him to transfer to his wheelchair—we got more expert at all of it. As we became more efficient and could better maximize his happiness in each day, that created room for me to take on something more. More for Lucas, but also more for kids like Lucas, more for awareness of Menkes syndrome.

To this day I can't honestly say how much of this was to busy myself into distraction and how much was motivated by a feeling that something had to change. It was both. Changing the long-term outcome for Lucas seemed nearly impossible. I felt the injustice of all this; not that it had happened in our family but that it happens at all to anyone. Couldn't our medical system do better? Surely some of this was avoidable—if not for Lucas then for the next generation of kids with a rare flaw in their genes.

It was nearly six years after Lucas's diagnosis that I felt maybe I could help do something about Menkes syndrome. I was only dimly aware that doing something could be "advocating." I was unsure exactly what an advocate was or did and if I could call myself one. I began by telling Lucas's story, first in blog posts and then in a short film called *Menkes Disease: Finding Help & Hope*, about my own family and two others who also had sons with Menkes. I remember procrastinating. Maybe I couldn't or shouldn't make the film. My wife and I kept putting off the time for our own interviews. When we were in low moods we couldn't muster the strength for it, and when we were in more positive moods we didn't want to risk ruining them by telling a tragic tale. But I kept coming back to the idea that there were so few Menkes syndrome families (I knew of about seventy), what chance was there that someone other than me both cared passionately about this condition and had the skill set to make a documentary? Within such a small community, it was impossible to kid myself. It was a stark example of "If not me, who?"

As I searched for places to share these stories of Lucas, I heard about an organization that brings together rare disease advocates called Global Genes. I doubted if I was the type of advocate that belonged at their conference. But then I submitted my first story about Lucas, and it won the Global Genes Rare Patient Story Award in 2015. I felt encouraged. After I was nominated as one of their Champions of Hope, I got further encouragement to attend their summit that year from the person who arranged their travel stipends. I mention this to show just how much pushing and encouragement it took for me to know I might belong in this club that no one wants to be a member of. I needed more than an invitation. I needed to be pulled in.

I had no idea that the people who were gathering every year at Global Genes were my people. That conference changed my world. Each person I met had a one in a million story. And nearly every one of them would open their hearts wide and retell the tale if you asked. So many unique stories, but nearly all of them were rooted in tragedy yet bursting with optimism, determination, and hope. I was most impressed with Bo Bigelow. His daughter Tess had just been diagnosed three months earlier. It had taken me nearly five years to get from diagnosis day to a conference for advocates. And here Bo was not only at the conference but already hosting a podcast about his daughter. Bo was proudly wearing his daughter's photo on his event lanyard to remind everyone of his "why" and to prompt conversations about her and the disorder she lives with: Hao-Fountain syndrome. This, by the way, is a technique I've stolen and now employ at every conference for rare disease I attend. You'll find a photo of a smiling Lucas captioned "Ask me about Menkes syndrome" added to my lanyard at each event.

I could feel myself going through mental growing pains at that conference. Not only because of the people I met, some of whom became lifelong friends and allies, but through the education presented at the panel discussions. I was introduced to so many different types of advocacy and different personal paths where each person played to the strengths they already had as they tried to build up new skills too.

People at the summit had held bake sales and 5Ks as fundraising events. Many were lobbying their legislatures at the state or national level to enact better policies. Some were gathering patient data to spur academics and industry to find new treatments. So many of them—despite being just a lay person parent like me—could speak the language of advanced genetic researchers. One rare dad's question has not stopped echoing in my ears in the nine years since. I can still see him looming over me. I'm pretty tall at six foot one. But he was bigger. The metaphoric implications of his greater size hit me: *He's bigger, more capable, more knowledgeable. There's so much I don't know.* His voice came from on high: "What's the length of the *ATP7A* gene?" *I don't know that.* I didn't even know what unit of measurement you'd use. Microns? But knowing the length of the *ATP7A* gene, the gene that causes Menkes syndrome, could help determine if gene therapy was possible. *Other people know this? Did I need to learn all this?* My imposter syndrome kicked into high gear. But so did my sense of what was possible—the many ways to advocate.

I was forced to reflect on what strengths I could bring to bear for rare disease. I knew it was neither running a 5K nor holding a bake sale. But I had run a film festival before, and I could help people make their rare disease stories into videos. I first did this two years later with Bo Bigelow, the fellow rare disease dad I met at that event. Since then we've together made several more rare disease documentaries and taught hundreds of others how they can do the same. And we launched DISORDER: The Rare Disease Film Festival and The DISORDER Channel dedicated to rare disease patient stories.

It's been nine years since my introduction to Global Genes and over three years since I joined their staff full-time, and I could not be prouder of the way our RARE Advocacy Summit continues to be a welcoming place for those looking to start their own path to improving the lives of those facing rare diseases. And the summit also remains a valuable place for more experienced advocates to advance their own knowledge and share that expertise with those newer to this life. We aim to meet each person where they are at. I'm fortunate to now be among the staff that make sure today's events have the same welcoming and encouraging effects they had on me when I was the newbie. In my opening remarks to first-timers, I explicitly point out that no one is an imposter. By virtue of showing up they are all advocates. I acknowledge that our event remains intimidating despite our best efforts. I warn first-timers that there will be both information overload and emotional overload.

And for the ones who don't feel ready yet to attend one of our events, I'm thrilled to have led the creation of an online community for Global Genes—our Facebook group. For those who can't attend our in-person events, this can be the way to "find your people."

Global Genes offers so many programs that can benefit the rare disease community:

Do you have a question and need to be connected to helpful resources? Email our RARE Concierge.

Do you feel medical students are not properly trained about the unique care needs for rare disease patients? You can participate in our RARE Compassion Program, which allows medical students to learn from those patients and families who have lived experience.

Are you a patient advocacy organization ready to collaborate with researchers or pharma? Our RARE Drug Development Symposium can guide you, and you can learn more about our Rare-X program's offerings for your community.

Do you want to make your rare disease story into a documentary? Watch our RAREly Told Stories training videos.

The single issue I hear about most from rare disease families is a feeling of isolation. With several years of experience, I can now offer a bit of advice to help end that feeling of isolation: You must find your people. I hope my work at Global Genes will always be informed by the memory that some of "our people" may need more than an invitation to join—they may need a gentle push, a pull, or a hand up. And if you haven't found your people yet, I'd be honoured to introduce you to some of them.

Daniel's son was diagnosed with Menkes syndrome, or Menkes disease.

Menkes disease (MD) is an inherited X-linked recessive disorder that affects many systems in the body. Affected infants are often born prematurely and may have non-specific symptoms such as hypothermia, hypoglycemia, and prolonged jaundice. One obvious and specific physical sign is "steely" or "kinky" hair that usually develops by several months of age. Menkes disease

is also associated with seizures, stunted growth, failure to thrive, unstable body temperature, and intellectual disability.
https://rarediseases.org/rare-diseases/menkes-disease/
Source: NORD

At the age of twelve months, **Daniel DeFabio's** first child, Lucas, was diagnosed with the rare disease Menkes syndrome. After adjusting his expectations of what raising a child might look like, Daniel began to tell Lucas's story in blogs, a podcast, and a short documentary. That film led to Daniel co-founding DISORDER: The Rare Disease Film Festival and later The Disorder Channel, both dedicated to spreading awareness for patient families facing any of the more than 10,000 rare diseases.

One of Daniel's stories about Lucas won the 2015 Rare Patient Story Award from Global Genes. His award-winning twelve-minute documentary on Menkes syndrome is narrated by Oscar nominee Mary McDonnell.

He has written for Courageous Parents Network, The Mighty, *RARE Revolution Magazine*, *Videomaker* magazine, Boing Boing, and *Geek* magazine. He currently works as Global Genes' director of community engagement. He lives in Ballston Spa, New York. More on Daniel can be found at www.thedisordercollection.com/danieldefabiospeaker.

Chapter 4: Seeing My Future Through Caregiving

By Erin Paterson

My husband was lying on the couch with his left leg extended. I was standing over him, about to remove his bandages for the first time. I didn't know how he was feeling in that moment, but I was afraid of what his knee would look like, and I was terrified of touching him in case I accidentally hurt him. I hesitantly unwrapped his knee, which was covered in a Tensor bandage, layers of gauze, and some sort of padding.

"How much of this stuff are we supposed to take off?" I asked him.

"I don't know," he said.

We referred to the inadequate printout the hospital had given us for post-operative care, then called my mom for advice. I continued removing the layers to find wrinkled skin, numerous incisions, and yellow bruising down his leg. My husband had undergone reconstructive knee surgery two days earlier and since then had spent his time on the couch with an ice pump attached to his leg. He was in pain and unable to move much, so I brought him his meals, his medication, and anything else he needed. I helped him shower, change his clothes, and get settled into bed at night. That type of hands-on care was always what I imagined caregiving to be. But in fact, I have been a caregiver for much longer than that—I just didn't label it that way.

For years I have been caring for my dad, who is living with Huntington's disease (HD). At first his needs were minimal. Just before the pandemic, he had lost his driver's licence and moved into a retirement home. Occasionally I would take him to the bank to deposit a cheque, help him update his phone, or take him shopping for new clothes. We live in different cities, so helping my dad is an all-day affair. I drive two hours north, spend a few hours with him and make the long drive home. At this point in time he was still able to carry on a conversation with me and would call me several times a week to chat.

As his disease progressed, it took away his abilities one little piece at a time, to the point that my dad now needs help with most aspects of daily living. Personal support workers come in several times a day to help him get dressed, brush his teeth and hair, make sure he is drinking enough water, and check he has not fallen and hurt himself. Behind the scenes, I am managing the rest of his life. This is an important job that I take very seriously. I am honoured to be able to do this for my dad and fortunate that he is accepting of my help, but it is also a huge responsibility. I order any supplies he needs, from shampoo and toothpaste to supplemental drinks and wipes. I make sure his walker is serviced. I get his glasses repaired (he has broken them four times this year alone). I pay his bills. I schedule his doctor appointments, go to them with him, and make sure he receives any necessary follow-up care. But the biggest and most time-consuming thing I do is advocate for my dad.

My dad is fully aware of what is going on in his life and what is happening to him, but he has almost completely lost the ability to speak. He can only say two or three words at a time, and it is incredibly difficult for him to spit them out. If you are speaking with him, you need to wait up to sixty seconds for a response, and as you can probably imagine, that doesn't happen when he finds himself in the emergency department after having had a fall. In many of his interactions with the medical system, staff are too impatient to wait for a response and often label him as non-verbal. This misinformation gets included in his medical records, which in turn perpetuates the problem as the next nurse on shift reads the notes and assumes it to be true. Much of my time is spent educating people, from doctors to nurses to PSWs, about Huntington's disease and how to interact with my dad.

It's best if you ask him questions he can give a yes or no answer to. Please ask him just one question at a time, and give him plenty of time to reply. Just because he is not making eye contact with you doesn't mean he isn't aware of what is going on. Yes he can make decisions for himself, but please keep me in the loop so I can make sure he gets the follow-up care you are requesting.

This year during a meeting with hospital staff, they kept trying to blame what my dad was going through on his Huntington's disease. This is a situation I encounter all the time. Unfortunately, my dad had broken his hip, and after it was fixed he was transferred to the rehab (physio) unit at his local hospital. I attended a family planning meeting at the beginning of his stay to discuss expected outcomes with the staff. One of the first things the physiotherapist said was she felt my dad would be safer in a wheelchair.

"I know he walks sort of funny. That is his normal gait," I told her. "I realize it might not look safe, but that is the way he has been walking for a long time, and we are okay with the risk. Any time he has fallen it has not been because of his shaky walk."

"We still think a wheelchair would be safer than him using his walker," she reiterated. This comment exasperated me, but I tried not to let my tone of voice betray it.

"I understand, but let's at least give him a shot. I would like for you to work on getting him back to his baseline and using his walker," I said before sharing some more details about my dad's abilities that I thought might be helpful for them to know. "His walk has a pattern. He kicks his right foot out every fourth step, and he can't control it. I have some videos of him walking if you would like to see them." For the past few years I have been taking videos of my dad walking to keep track of his movements and help determine if his HD medications are working. They have come in handy on more than one occasion.

I don't know where I get the bravery to speak up for my dad, as I am not a naturally outspoken person. But I think in that situation it came down to how frustrated I felt that they were underestimating him and not even giving him a chance to do better. They were passing judgment on his abilities based on the rundown state they found him in after one of the worst moments of his life and their preconceived ideas of what an eighty-year-old with HD looks like. I realize that is the nature of the medical system, so I did my best to speak up for him and paint a picture of what his life was like before he was admitted. "He was playing shuffleboard the day before he broke his hip. He was walking down to the dining hall from the third floor with his walker. We want to get him back to that," I told them. "He is still pretty active, all things considered."

Two months later when my dad was discharged and went back to his retirement home, there was a big adjustment period for us both. He was trying to get his strength back, and I was making constant phone calls to set up the necessary services and adjust them as needed. Checking in to make sure his prescription was faxed over from the hospital, that the nurse was coming to do his wound care, that the personal support workers were arriving at their scheduled times. It took weeks for things to settle down to a new normal.

Even when things are fairly stable, I spend a lot of time trying to determine if something I have been told is accurate. Is it a need of my dad's or a need for the staff, who don't want to do their jobs? Is it a concern of my dad's or of the personal support worker? We all have our own opinions and interpret things differently, so just because something is brought up by one person doesn't mean I need to act on it. On one of my recent visits, a PSW flagged me down in the hallway and told me I needed to order my dad some special shoes.

"I can barely get his shoes on," she said as she walked with me down the hall.

"Did you see the slip-ons I bought him?" I asked her.

"Yes, but the back collapses when I put them on and my finger gets stuck."

"There is a shoehorn in the closet," I told her, thinking she might not have known it was there.

"He shakes too much for me to use that." She stopped walking so she could pull out her phone and look up a pair of shoes online that she thought would be appropriate. "You should get him these."

I took a look at the beige Velcro shoes on the screen she was holding out for me to see.

"Thank you so much. I will think about that," I told her, but I was not convinced. I asked multiple people, and since no one else was having that problem, I didn't buy the expensive shoes.

Being a caregiver involves answering emails and text messages. Having phone call after phone call. Discussing what's happening with my husband and brother and trying to figure out the best path forward for my dad. The tasks ebb and flow depending on how well my dad is doing. There is no predicting when he will need me, but when he does I drop everything to do what needs to be done.

In the past five years as his needs have increased, this has taken its toll on me. I have gained a lot of weight, I have been battling depression, I am having a lot of trouble with anxiety, and I feel like I am constantly at my limit. I am not saying these things are happening just because of my dad, but being his caregiver adds a lot of pressure to my life. Especially because I know I am going to get Huntington's one day too.

I have gone through genetic testing, and I tested gene positive for HD. This means it is with 100 percent certainty that I will also develop the disease. Living with this knowledge is extremely hard, and it adds an extra layer to being a caregiver because helping my dad is a trigger for me. Every time I get a phone call, my first reaction is panic and fear. Every email I answer is a reminder of what is going to happen to me. Every time I visit my dad, I am seeing my own future.

Sometimes I am able to handle the pressures of being a caregiver with no problem; other times it can be exceedingly difficult. So I have had to come up with ways of coping. If a phone call gets me into a state of panic, I try to take the time to do a ten-minute meditation. If I am dealing with back-to-back issues, I make sure I don't miss my workout at the gym. If I am feeling low on energy, I go for a walk at my local nature trail. If a simple task like ordering body wash off Amazon is freaking me out, it is a signal that things are getting to be too much for me, so I ask my husband for help. If I am overwhelmed, I try to reach out to a friend.

I remember one particular call I had with a girlfriend a while back when my dad was just starting to decline. "I have to go buy some pants for my dad, but it's freaking me out. I don't know why I keep delaying it. I should just do it and get it over with," I told her. Every time I thought of going to the store I would start to panic.

"That's because it's not just about pants, Erin," she said so matter-of-factly. I thought this was the strangest comment.

"What do you mean?" I asked, completely confused.

"It is a representation of what your dad can no longer do, and that is a hard thing to deal with."

"Ahhhh. I didn't think of that. Thank you." There I was beating myself up when there was actually more to it. I got off the call with a better understanding of how I was feeling. Even so, there are times when I don't call a friend for support because I just want to deal with the situation and move on as quickly as possible. Sometimes talking about it prolongs everything, but if I don't talk to someone I can start to feel isolated and alone. It's a very fine line.

And sometimes my coping methods are just not enough. There have been times when nothing helps and I can't find my way out of the panic I feel. Where no matter how hard I try to change my mindset and look at things from a positive point of view, I simply can't. Where the act of meditation is too hard because it requires me to change. Where no amount of box breathing will help. Those are the times when I just need to give in. When I let the overwhelm encompass me and I break down crying and then take a long nap, even if it is the middle of the afternoon. I guess that in itself is a form of self-care, the giving in to the emotions. At some point in time I have to allow myself to feel and process my emotions. But it is a tricky thing to balance because it is very easy to let those emotions consume me, and it can be incredibly difficult to pull myself back out of that cycle of despair.

For too long my needs and well-being have taken a back seat to the needs of others. It was not something that happened intentionally—I was just trying to do my best for everyone. Now I know I can no longer sustain that. It is unhealthy, and my body is already paying the price. So I am doing my best to change that habit. I'm learning to listen to my body and trying to take care of myself. I think the biggest part of that for me is learning how to release the guilt of not accomplishing enough in a day. Trying not to beat myself up when I feel I haven't done enough at work, at home, for my family, and for my dad. Allowing myself to have some downtime, especially after a particularly hard day as a caregiver. Not always focusing on just pushing forward at all costs. But this is a constant challenge for me, made evident by a conversation I had with my husband this week, the second week of caring for him after his surgery. I flew into the house after getting some groceries and made him lunch before heading off to the gym. When I got back he said, "You are always in and out, in and out. Do you realize how busy you are?"

"Really? What? No, this is just my everyday life. You are just home to see it now," I told him.

Clearly if I can't even realize how busy I am, then I have work to do.

Being a caregiver is a challenge, and sometimes I am angry that this is a role I need to fulfill. But I feel closer to my dad now than I have in my entire life, and that truly is a gift. When the inevitable happens and he finally succumbs to this disease, I will know I have done my best for my dad, that his life was enriched because of my help. And I will live with no regrets.

Erin is a caregiver for her dad who is living with Huntington's disease.

Huntington's disease is a genetic, progressive, neurodegenerative disorder characterized by the gradual development of involuntary muscle movements affecting the hands, feet, face, and trunk and progressive deterioration of cognitive processes and memory (dementia). Neurologic movement abnormalities may include uncontrolled, irregular, rapid, jerky movements (chorea) and athetosis, a condition characterized by relatively slow, writhing involuntary movements. Dementia is typically associated with progressive disorientation and confusion, personality disintegration, impairment of memory control, restlessness, agitation, and other symptoms and findings. In individuals with the disorder, disease duration may range from approximately 10 years up to 25 years or more. Life-threatening complications may result from pneumonia or other infections, injuries related to falls, or other associated developments.
https://rarediseases.org/rare-diseases/huntingtons-disease/
Source: NORD

Erin Paterson is a published author, public speaker, and Huntington's disease advocate. She was diagnosed as gene positive for Huntington's disease in her early thirties. Shortly after, she started suffering from depression, then received more crushing news—she was infertile. Despite those diagnoses, she was determined to have a family and live a joyful life.

Erin is on a mission to positively impact other people's lives by writing and speaking about genetic disease, depression, and infertility. She shows that it is possible to live a meaningful life even when faced with unexpected obstacles. She is the author of *All Good Things: A Memoir About Genetic Testing, Infertility, and One Woman's Relentless Search for Happiness* and *Huntington's Disease Heroes: Inspiring Stories of Resilience from the HD Community*. Erin is also the founder of Lemonade Press, a publisher focused on empowering people from under-represented medical communities by helping them write and share their own journeys in inspiring anthologies.

She lives in Toronto with her husband and daughter. Learn more about Erin at https://www.erinpaterson.com/ and on Instagram @erinpaterson_allgoodthings.

Chapter 5: A Walking Rarity

By Tessa Koller

Saturday, May 14, 2022

I was certain I was feeling better and well enough to leave my house. On that spring morning, I was hungry to create something, a feeling I hadn't had in months. It was on my schedule to spend the afternoon doing some shopping and then drawing later in the day. Sitting at my kitchen island counter, I sipped green tea and penned my shopping list in preparation for a trip to the art store known as Blick.

The clock on my stove ticked on to 11:45, and I slid my wool coat over my shoulders and zipped my list in my purse. Braving the cold, I walked outside, and gusts of wind whirled around me. I ducked into my stepfather's car, and we made the thirty-minute commute.

When we got to the store, Paul dropped me off in front and I bustled into the building. Inside, warmth blanketed my body and I felt more and more like me. Those subtle smells of paint fumes and cedarwood from pencils ignited me with the creative energy I thrived on. I yanked a cart away from the wall and pushed it towards the watercolour aisle. Watercolour paints were neatly hanging along one half of the aisle, and I selected burnt sienna and nature-toned colours.

Turning the corner, I found specialty branded pencils, erasers, and other items for drawing. I reached for a package of tools for blending graphite and charcoal on the top shelf. I outstretched my arm and a pang in my stomach caused me to hunch forward. Bracing my forehead on my wrist, I practised diaphragmatic breathing to ease the tension. Heat rose up my chest, neck, and face. My face was splotchy red.

"Now is not the time," I mumbled.

I repeated that phrase when symptoms were coming on. Maybe I wasn't fully recovered from the culprit that had me bedridden two months prior. I'd been out of bed for only four days and probably should've waited a week. I stopped *should*-ing myself and continued wheeling my cart forward.

The next aisle held an assortment of paper—from smooth to fine tooth to textured surfaces. Again, I reached for the top shelf and felt a second shooting pain in my stomach. Agitated, I finally went to the ladies room and parked my cart outside the door, hoping nobody would move it. Plunging into the stall, my chest tightened as if a force were squeezing the soul out of me. A familiar fear resurfaced, the fear that my health would constantly interfere with and ruin special occasions or moments with friends and family.

Something else is wrong, I thought, as I started vomiting blood. Symptoms are like warning sirens. Seeing red was an indicator of a deeper problem. Our bodies aren't the enemy, but mine was the antagonist in my story, and I let out a sigh of frustration. Pressing two fingers to my neck, I felt my heart pounding and fluttering.

I rested my head on the dank steel wall and then quickly peeled it away at the thought of how many germs might be on there. My heart rate went from erratic to oddly faint. Palpitations weren't abnormal, but my slowing pulse was. Fatigue set in my body like it was hardening cement, stiffening my muscles and bones. It felt as though my blood was boiling.

The pounding sensations in my chest reminded me of how I was born with congenital heart disease and how it has been a struggle since my birth. At ten weeks old, I underwent emergency open heart surgery to patch-repair a ventricular septal defect and relieve a vascular ring strangulation around my esophagus, trachea, and aortic arch. Within the year following my surgery, I experienced developmental delays and couldn't sit, stand, walk, or talk. Because of a deficient immune system, I was vulnerable to repeated infections and illnesses.

By the time I was nine months of age, my mother noticed me drawing on my high-chair tray using my pointer finger, a sign my fine motor skills were emerging. She recognized that drawing could facilitate my focus and concentration and develop my visual voice.

Her advocacy introduced me to art therapy, the foundation for the success I now have as an artist, clothing designer, and writer.

Throughout my elementary and middle school education, I dealt with physical, mental, and emotional struggles that required outside therapies to strengthen my areas of weakness. My mother sought counsellors and tutors to assist me with my language and cognitive processing difficulties. Programs away from home, like summer camp in Canada and a boarding school in Southern Illinois called Brehm, prepared me for independent living. Private instruction and daily journalling unlocked my potential and helped me realize my capabilities.

From Brehm, I attained a four-year scholarship to an art college in Milwaukee, the Milwaukee Institute of Art and Design. But it wasn't until 2008, my last semester of college, that I suffered a dizzy spell and fainted in my drawing studio during class. One second I was standing in front of a wall and drawing in black charcoal on a large sheet of paper. The next I was unconscious on the floor. The episode prompted the transferring of my health care to Milwaukee's medical system, where I met a cardiologist who specialized in structural and congenital heart disease.

During my first consultation, the cardiologist asked if I knew about the genetic syndrome DiGeorge syndrome, now 22q11.2 deletion syndrome. Six weeks later, I learned that 22q was the mystery behind my multitude of illnesses. That means that for twenty-four years, I didn't know I had 22q and labelled myself a walking malfunction. The diagnosis sent me into a spiralling depression, and I feared my life was ending. It was another pivotal turning point that led to intensive counselling so I could gain a better understanding of myself and my health condition.

22q11.2 deletion syndrome is a microdeletion, or deleted genes, from a section of the twenty-second chromosome, affecting every system down the centre of the body. The syndrome comes with more than two hundred associated conditions and diseases. Although living with the syndrome posed many threats to my well-being, it has also been a source of inspiration in my artwork. A portfolio of paintings I produced one year after my diagnosis of 22q was an abstract series combining body organs and floral structures bursting with vivid colour and energetic compositions.

Over a decade later, during the COVID-19 pandemic, I seriously pursued drawing and painting using my health as a subject matter.

Not surprisingly, I caught COVID-19 three times and experienced more than twenty-five emergency room visits and medical episodes that could've easily ended my existence. Aside from my physical health struggles, my mental health has played a role in exacerbating symptoms as well. It's amazing how overpowering anxiety and depression can be.

Automatic negative thoughts came more easily to me than anything else did. My passion for art, however, was much stronger. Creativity was my constant companion and silenced my noisy mind. A pencil and a blank sheet of paper instilled a sense of magic and could make my negative thoughts disappear. Drawing especially abolished my faulty belief systems about myself and restored my self-esteem.

While depression and anxiety may seem more powerful than I am at times, art infuses me with hope. Whether I produce a portrait of a rock star or an animal, or an abstract painting, I feel an enormous sense of accomplishment. Creating makes me feel good, and that's why I was at the art store that day, to feel good again.

Pulling myself together, I headed to the sink, turned on the faucet, and splashed cold water on my face. I walked out into the hallway and took a sip at the fountain. Reclaiming my cart, I called it quits and ambled to the checkout counter. My heart palpitations returned vigorously and then abruptly decreased. Waves of dizziness almost knocked me off balance, and I grasped the ledge of a shelf. The paintbrushes shook from their hooks as I tried to stabilize myself.

My breathing was shortening and tightening like someone was strapping me into a corset. I peered at the man behind the register, who wasn't assisting any other customers. When I got to the checkout counter, I sluggishly unloaded my cart and waited for the gentleman to bag my supplies. Ignoring his jabbering, I kept my two fingers on my wrist and nonchalantly counted my heartbeats.

Now is not the time.

Looking out the wall-sized window, I spotted my stepfather waiting for me. After the cashier wrapped everything up, he waved me off with "Enjoy your day making beautiful art!"

Not going to happen, Buddy.

Blood crept up my esophagus and I forcibly swallowed it down, scrunching my lips at the sting in my throat. I hauled four white bags to Paul's car, threw them into the trunk, and reclined in the passenger side seat, panting and out of breath. Paul assessed me with a concerned expression, noticing my extreme exhaustion.

"Can you just count my heart rate?" I begged, trying not to cry or panic.

He gripped my wrist and stared off into space, counting to himself.

A minute passed.

"It's very low," he confirmed.

Paul drove me back home, and when he pulled into our driveway, I staggered into my house in search of my mother. As I hobbled up the stairs and into my parents' bedroom, she rushed towards me, grabbing my arms and then touching my clammy forehead. Talking hurt my scratchy, constricted throat. Symptoms were piling on, leaving me unable to verbalize the order in which they were occurring. Drifting in and out of consciousness, I couldn't read my pulse at all or understand what was happening to me.

When the paramedics arrived, I was fearing I wouldn't get through the day. Then I repeated that awful phrase, but this time, changing one word:

"Now is not *my* time. Now is not *my* time . . ."

Two burly men hoisted me onto the gurney, securing my ankles and holding my arms down so I wouldn't roll off. In the ambulance, I overheard the driver reciting my raging symptoms on the phone to a doctor at the hospital.

"Severely distended abdomen, and swelling noted in the ankles and feet. Heart rate of thirty-two, and she is exhibiting signs of—"

Then, I blacked out.

After I regained consciousness, I was in the emergency room hooked up to an IV and listening to the nurse report my symptoms like she was reporting the local news. The overseeing doctor had diagnosed me with pancreatitis, a disease not associated with 22q. On top of having the genetic condition, I had postural orthostatic tachycardia syndrome, or POTS, a diagnosis I received in 2018. POTS is a secondary condition not related to 22q—just another monster to deal with.

POTS causes light-headedness, fainting, and irregular blood pressure and heart rate after extended periods of standing or sitting. The countless number of health issues I endure daily is almost unmanageable, and in the emergency room, I felt like I was trying to win yet another battle against my own body. I knew I needed to stop fighting against myself.

At 8:00 in the evening, the nurse released me from the hospital with a list of instructions to follow to reduce inflammation and resolve the pancreatitis. Back at home that night, I curled up with my grey tabby cat and went to bed early.

The very next morning, I uprooted my Vitamix blender from a shelf in my garage where my mother stowed large kitchen appliances. I blended spinach, cucumber, blueberries, and celery, my favourite go-to smoothie for reducing inflammation. Smoothies cooled my body down and aided digestion. I poured the smoothie into a silver canteen and drank it throughout the morning and afternoon.

Although I wasn't fully recovered, I engaged in activities that promoted wellness. Healing and perseverance derive from my willingness to access internal and external resources. External resources include counselling, building meaningful friendships in my community, doing yoga, and meditating. My internal resources are my artistic abilities, which allow me to reach a mindful acceptance of who I am and the realization that my genetic disorder doesn't own me. I am not 22q or the sum of my differences.

Sustaining a strong mindset made me feel much better. I was thinking about my upcoming travels to Europe with the International 22q11.2 Foundation, an organization dedicated to supporting those with 22q and providing up-to-date research on the syndrome. Having 22q and sharing my story gifted me opportunities to travel worldwide to places such as Canada, Ireland, Italy, and Croatia to speak at scientific family meetings. I've dedicated almost fifteen years of my life to raising awareness of 22q in the media. I've co-hosted fashion show fundraisers and gallery exhibitions showcasing my creations. Being an advocate is as fulfilling as being an artist; it makes me want to keep going. Keep creating. Keep giving.

The diagnosis of 22q unveiled my purpose and helped me love myself more. This new-found self-love formed through my advocacy and from connecting with others also facing chronic health challenges. Art and advocacy fuel me with inner strength and empowerment and greatly improve my mental health. With that in mind, I cleaned off my drawing table and assembled my wooden easel. I unpacked the coloured pencils I purchased from the art store, grabbed a fresh pad of paper, and drew a portrait of a tiger.

Tessa is living with 22q11.2 deletion syndrome.

22q11.2 deletion syndrome (DS) is a chromosomal anomaly that causes a congenital malformation disorder whose common features include cardiac defects, palatal anomalies, facial dysmorphism, developmental delay, and immune deficiency.

https://rarediseases.org/mondo-disease/22q11-2-deletion-syndrome/

Source: NORD

Tessa Koller is an artist and author living in St. Charles, Illinois. She holds a bachelor of fine arts degree from the Milwaukee Institute of Art and Design, where she studied creative writing, drawing, and painting. At the age of twenty-four, Tessa was diagnosed with the rare genetic disorder 22q11.2 deletion syndrome, and she has congenital heart disease, lung disease, and other associated health conditions. Since 2010, she has travelled to dozens of countries and spoken publicly about her challenges and triumphs with 22q. Today, she draws stunning portraits of domestic pets and wildlife and is published in multiple wellness magazines and journals. To learn more about Tessa's art and story, follow her on Instagram @tessakollerart.

Chapter 6: Perseverance and Hope with a Rare Illness

By Joe Kammers

Trigger warning: This chapter briefly mentions self-harm.

One morning I woke up with severe cramping in my legs. My initial assumption was that I had gotten too cold overnight with the air conditioning on. I've had muscle cramps off and on over the years from sports injuries. I tried what I thought would help best, including massages, Epsom soaks, and Tensor bandages. When the cramps still hadn't gone away after a few days, I made my way to urgent care, since my primary doctor was booked out for a month. That was the beginning of a diagnosis that changed my life.

In urgent care, they did all the initial tests, only to come back that I was "most likely" dehydrated and I should pick up some Pedialyte or Gatorade on the way home and follow up with my primary doctor as soon as I could. About three weeks into having severe pain, I was finally able to get into my primary. He did some physical tests and blood tests, but we would have to wait for the results to see if anything came back abnormal. After a couple of days' wait, my primary doctor noticed my creatine kinase levels were extremely high, which can indicate skeletal muscle degeneration, and a referral was put in to see a neurologist.

I was in pain every day, and I grew more impatient, exhausted, and irritable as I waited to see a specialist. It reflected at home, at work, and everywhere I went. I just wanted an answer and to be treated. When my appointment finally came, the neurologist did more extensive physical testing and set up an EMG (electromyography) test to "listen" to my muscles. Little did I know, that was going to be one of the most painful tests I have ever been through.

I entered a standard medical room and was instructed to lie on the table in my hospital gown. Starting at my foot, the doctor placed two needles a couple of inches apart and sent an electrical current through the needles. A speaker would make a sound when my muscles contracted. This continued all the way from the top of my foot to each main muscle up my legs, back, neck, and arms. I had no idea what the length or pitch of the sounds meant. But I felt the pain of the process. The test took about forty-five excruciating minutes to complete. The results came back as "some form of myopathy," but nothing definitive. Just as I was starting to get answers, my employer's insurance changed and this doctor along with the clinic was no longer in the network, so frustratingly, I had to start again.

I found a new clinic and primary care provider. Then I had to wait to be seen, wait to explain what had been going on, and wait again to finally see neurology. All that time I was still in pain, still with no finite answer. I had people telling me, "It's probably all in your head." Hearing that really upset me because it wasn't in my head. The pain was real, and I knew something was wrong. Activities I used to do with ease were now a struggle. This had been going on for around four months by now, and my mental health was really starting to deteriorate as well. All I wanted to do was sleep and hope the pain went away. I wanted to not feel fatigued, to not want to nap in the middle of the day because I was so exhausted. I wanted the pain to stop so much that I considered hurting myself, but I couldn't because of the support of my family. I just wanted some positive news.

A new neurologist came along who was much more personable and more open to listening to me than the last one. I was starting to feel good. After my initial examination with him as well as going over all my old test results, he had a diagnosis! I knew a diagnosis meant the possibility of bad news, but it was good to hear he knew what was wrong: myotonic muscular dystrophy (MMD). "There is no cure, but there is treatment that can make quality of life better," he explained. During the appointment, he also told me MMD is a rare disease that eventually causes muscular degradation and decreases life expectancy. He immediately started me on some medication and a treatment plan from that point on. I started the medication but was warned that too much use could cause gum decay, and I would need to wean myself off it if I ever chose to stop. *It doesn't matter. I'm finally getting somewhere*, I said to myself.

I started doing further research, looking for MMD organizations that offered clinical trials I could possibly take part in. I joined a few support groups and started communicating with other people, even finding out one of my friends had gone to high school with another gentleman with the same disease. We connected on Facebook to support each other. My healing was just starting to begin when I hit another roadblock.

My insurance changed again!

Eager to get some answers, I found a new clinic and a new neurologist. *At least I have a diagnosis this time around, so continuing treatment shouldn't be an issue.* I received the referral and to my shock, I was able to get in within a week to see neurology. At my first appointment with my new neurologist, he started looking at all of my records and checking my meds. His first question to me was "Does the medication seem like it has been helping?"

"Honestly, it hasn't," I told him. "It's been more an adjustment of my lifestyle that seems to improve my quality of life." His recommendation was to stop the medication since it could do more harm than good if it wasn't helping. I agreed with him, and we set up a plan to wean off. The second statement he made was that if I had come to him twenty years ago, he would have given me the same diagnosis (MMD), but he wanted to do genetic testing just to be sure. He explained that the genetic test was so specific it could rule out certain conditions but also alert ones that were never thought of, which would be important if I ever wanted children. After he explained the benefits, I agreed to go through genetic testing.

Then the world came to a stop. COVID-19 hit and all non-essential appointments were made virtual, and guess what, a genetic test for a non-emergency is considered non-essential. Knowing this was delayed did upset me a little, but I knew I was finally going to get answers. There was something larger than me going on in the world, and I knew I had to be patient. Insurance complications also made it harder, so my neurologist's nurse practitioner started to look for an alternative way for me to get this done. They were able to send me a home testing kit, which was as simple as a mouth swab. I sent in the sample but was told it might take longer for the results since this lab also did COVID testing. A few months later the results came back, and I set up a virtual appointment.

I was sitting in my living room with my spouse, surrounded by our four dogs, for the call. My wife was probably more nervous than I was since I was used to getting no answers. My neurologist, who was calling from the hospital, apologized immediately that we had to do this virtually because of COVID, and he wished he could have given me this news in person. My heart dropped. "Is it something worse?" I asked. He explained that the gene that would normally indicate MMD issues was normal. Instead, two other genes showed mutations: One was *RYR1*, which can cause susceptibility to malignant hyperthermia, but that should not be causing my symptoms. The second was *PKHA1*, which indicated that glycogen storage disease IXd (GSD9D) was causing my issues. After a rundown of how genetics works—thankfully I retained some information from high school biology—he got to the point of telling me how rare this is. There are only about forty to fifty known cases worldwide. Even he had to research what he could, since there is not much literature on it. He said he would send me copies of his research.

Being misdiagnosed upset me greatly, but knowing I now had a good doctor on my side, I knew I could push through this. While the diagnosis wasn't what I had hoped for, considering there is no cure or treatment, I knew I had to move forward with my life. Being a science nerd and trusting 100 percent in genetic testing, I knew this was what was wrong. I just needed to find the resources, with the backing of my medical team, as well as advocate for myself. I consider myself more of a pessimistic person, but for some reason this diagnosis gave me the courage to continue on and try to find others like me. Since that meeting, I have connected with a few other people with this disease. It was scary in the beginning knowing how rare I was, but after meeting others, I knew we could work with each other to compare treatments as well as other possibilities.

My neurologist suggested I watch for clinical studies that may come up for GSD9D, as well as find research organizations for rare diseases and support groups. Finally, we developed my treatment plan, as there are other types of GSDs with similar issues. First he wanted to check on my liver and heart, as those are very important organs that could be affected by my disease. The second step was to connect with the genetics department at the local children's hospital, since the other GSDs tend to affect children.

With the life-changing news, I went ahead with what he said and got all the appointments booked, somehow all in the same day, but I still had about a month to wait. That's when my personal research began. I ended up finding some clinical studies for other GSDs but not my specific one. I also found a group on Facebook for another rare disease, McArdle's, which apparently is somewhat similar as both cause muscle cells to not be able to break down glycogen, a complex sugar in foods. I was starting to feel some relief that I'd found some rare disease groups, especially when I discovered one with my specific GSD. Unfortunately, as expected, no one had any really good answers.

I also took that time to inform my family of my diagnosis. I explained how typically only males are affected, since the disease is linked to the X chromosome, and both parents need to carry the gene. This eased my amazing wife's and my mind about having a child—odds are, our child would not have to deal with this.

I attended my medical appointments as scheduled. I had to wear a Holter monitor for a couple of days to see how my heart was working, followed up by an ultrasound of my heart. I also had a series of blood tests to check my liver function as well as an ultrasound on my liver. My heart and liver were fine. That was a relief! Next up was the children's hospital visit.

At the genetic clinic at the children's hospital, there were kid-sized chairs and medical equipment as well as parents of children. In my mid-thirties I felt out of place, but I was treated with nothing but respect from all of the staff. I was just another patient, and they were super amazing when it came to making me feel comfortable, starting with when it was time to check my height and weight. After that, three people walked into the exam room: a genetic counsellor, an advanced practice nurse prescriber, and a nutritionist. They were all very excited to meet me. One even said, "I never thought I would ever meet someone with your version of this disease, so this is a great opportunity to learn from you." Hearing that made me feel very welcome because they took the time to research as much as they could into my disease as well as having learned something about it in medical school.

As the appointment went on, they explained more about my disease and how it has some similarities to other GSDs, and we started a plan of attack. The biggest change would be to adjust my diet to a high-protein diet, targeting around 140 grams per day. I was given a list of high-protein foods. They also referred me for physical therapy.

Once again, they said there's not much known about this disease, so everything would be a trial-and-error process.

The trial-and-error comment caught me off guard, but after thinking about it, that's what I was doing myself. I had never tried acupuncture before, but that seemed to help. I knew massage helped, as well as limiting the "new" movement of muscles on a daily basis: no heavy object movements, insane workouts, or anything my body was not used to. So I was mentally ready to go down this road.

I changed my diet and felt super bloated for the first few weeks until I found a steady plan that works for me. My diet basically consists of meat and dairy to reach this level. One palm-sized piece of meat for lunch and dinner, lots of yogurt or cheese, and protein shakes to help supplement. It took a little to get used to, but now I plan out everything to meet their criteria. I went to physical therapy but eventually stopped because I did not feel it had any benefit and I didn't want to continue adding to my medical bills.

I went back to see my primary for the first time since my official diagnosis. She was super happy that I finally got the results I needed. She said she entered my disease in the clinic's database so it can be referenced if I ever needed to go to the ER or for anything there.

I continued to make life adjustments, even trying a workout place with my wife to get somewhat active besides just walking the dogs. And we felt comfortable enough to try for a child. If I had what I was originally misdiagnosed with, we would have been risking our child's health. After six months of trying, we found out we needed to try fertility treatments. It was a combination of both of us, so there were going to be more tests in my life, but it would be worth it for a baby.

Time goes by, and I follow up with my specialist team after a year. There is nothing new, no changes, let's follow up in a year again, they said.

During this time, my wife and I were pretty much at the end of our intrauterine inseminations (IUIs), a fertility treatment that injects my sperm into my wife's Fallopian tubes at a specific time to achieve a pregnancy. We couldn't afford to continue treatments. Then an opportunity came around on a local radio station to win free IVF treatments, so we entered! We used one of our dogs to make a video, which consisted of him stating our history and why we wanted a child. I did the voice of our dog, and we also had family members and friends do short testimonials on why we should win IVF treatment. We were the lucky winners.

Part of the treatment was an option for a genetic test for more common genetic mutations, which we decided to go with, mainly because of my known issues, but also because we didn't know whether my wife had any issues. Humorously, they did tests for more common GSDs, which we were all fine for. All of the blood, sweat, and tears were worth it when my wife became pregnant with a baby girl. Nine months later, we held our beautiful girl in our arms, and I couldn't be more excited to be a father.

As I write this, my daughter is eight months old and doing amazing. But as she gets bigger, I tend to struggle more. I can feel my muscles getting weaker and sore. She loves to roughhouse and play with me all the time but also has her days of wanting only to be held. My body is not used to handling more weight than a laptop, so this has been very tough on me. I have my good days and bad days, but my wife is always there to support me and help me whenever she can. As my daughter grows, physically and developmentally, my body gets pushed in different ways, which causes excruciating pain. I dread not being able to keep up with her as she gets older. Not being able to interact in ways she wants me to. My wife is super supportive and said she will learn to understand. And I just need to continue to be there for her, which I plan on doing.

After years of pain, physical and mental, I can take a lot. I always idolized superheroes growing up—most of them had genetic mutations, and I always wanted a superpower too. Little did I know that I would find out I was a mutant along with these heroes. It took me a long time to figure out my superpower, and I discovered it is persistence. If I wasn't persistent in advocating for myself to get answers, I wouldn't have any. Now I want to spread my superpower to others and help them self-advocate.

This journey was by no means easy, and I know it won't get any easier, but thankfully my amazing wife, child, family, and current medical team are always there to support me. I know I couldn't have done it without them.

Joe is living with glycogen storage disease 9D.

Glycogen storage disease 9D is a benign form of phosphorylase kinase deficiency caused by variants in PHKA1, characterized by exercise intolerance, myalgia, muscle cramps, myoglobinuria, and progressive

muscle weakness.
https://rarediseases.org/mondo-disease/glycogen-storage-disease-ixd/
Source: NORD

Joe Kammers is forty years old and lives in Milwaukee, Wisconsin. He has a wife, a daughter, three dogs, three cats, and a pet snake. He spends most of his time navigating through fatherhood while watching his young one grow. When he has free time, he enjoys listening to music, watching movies (primarily fantasy), and playing video games. Joe also volunteers his time to the Global Gene's Rare Compassion program, working with student doctors to help them learn from the point of view of someone with a rare disease and what it took to get diagnosed.

Chapter 7: One Step at a Time

By Kimi Sorensen

One night when I was eleven years old, I was sitting at the island table, doing my homework next to my sister, when she asked me a question. She had to do a family tree for her seventh-grade class and include any medical conditions anyone in our family had. "Can I put that you have hydrocephalus on there?" she asked. I told her she couldn't put it on her family tree, "because I don't really feel like I have it, and I don't want anybody to know," I said. But then I started thinking, *Do I really "have" hydrocephalus?* I never had headaches, and we never talked about it. I never saw a neurosurgeon (probably not the best idea). In fact, whenever I mentioned it to my mom, she said, "You may not even need the shunt anymore. They will probably never take it out, but who knows."

Looking back now, I believe she said this for my own comfort. She didn't want me worrying about potential surgeries, if they might never happen, because that's really the truth with hydrocephalus. You have no idea when surgery will be needed. You can look at all of the statistics and percentages, but in reality, you have no idea.

Hydrocephalus is a neurological condition where there is an abnormal accumulation of cerebrospinal fluid in the ventricles of the brain. The excess fluid causes pressure and prevents the brain from growing. Without treatment, it is fatal. The standard treatment for the past seventy-five years has been a shunt—a valve connected to a tube that diverts the spinal fluid to a different part of the body, most commonly the peritoneal cavity.

There are many things that can and do go wrong with shunts every day that we cannot control. They can get clogged with calcium buildup, the tube can become so old that it breaks, the valve part of the shunt can malfunction, or you can get an infection, which is always scary since it involves multiple systems, because the distal part of the catheter can go in several different places throughout your body.

Growing up, I didn't necessarily feel really different from my peers at all, because I had been this way my entire life. I believe my mom wanted it to stay that way. Because of the way they handled it, I got to enjoy my childhood and not be constantly worried about a possible malfunction—I could just have fun.

In the pediatric population, it is estimated that 50 percent of shunts fail every year. When a shunt fails, different symptoms develop depending on the person's age. When a baby has a buildup of fluid on the brain, their head can expand because the skull has not completed growing. The excess fluid can also cause vomiting and a buildup of pressure behind the eyes, which can cause swelling of the optic nerves. An older person experiences many of the same symptoms; however, their head does not expand because the skull is finished growing, so they just get horrible headaches, since that fluid has nowhere to go. It's like a balloon that's being overfilled except it cannot pop.

Off and on throughout my life, I began to realize I was different from other people, even though my illness didn't automatically come to mind. But there has been this one little quirk about me I could never quite figure out. Honestly, if I knew more about hydrocephalus at the time, I probably would have put my finger on it, but fortunately I had no memories of hydrocephalus being a problem.

In one sense I feel lucky because I didn't know anything different than the incredible life I was already living. But in other ways, I sort of feel guilty now because I feel as if I didn't know how lucky I was. Maybe I would have enjoyed it more. That's the way we are with most things though, right? We don't realize how good we have it until it's gone.

When I was a sophomore in high school, I started having headaches. Yes, I had had the typical headaches as a child, but they always went away when I took medicines—but these didn't. When they stopped responding to medications, I didn't automatically think about my hydrocephalus. To be completely honest, I didn't even know enough about hydrocephalus to really connect the two.

Eventually, a complication was discovered that my doctor has seen in people who had been shunted a long time, called slit ventricle syndrome. This is where the ventricles in your brain are literally stuck shut. If you can imagine a balloon, when you blow air into it, it gets bigger. If you inhale the air back, the balloon starts to go flat, and eventually you can't bring in any more air without completely collapsing the balloon. It's the same idea here, but that was happening to the ventricles in my brain. When we learned of this complication, the doctor told us about a procedure he wanted to try, but he wanted to wait until my shunt malfunctioned again, because the surgery is far less painful if the ventricles are large.

Three months later, I had severe pain again and my doctor admitted me to the hospital. Again he mentioned the surgery, but he said, "I don't want to do it unless she has a malfunction and her ventricles are already big." About a week into my hospitalization, that happened and he did the surgery.

The procedure worked in the sense that it made my ventricles enlarge a little—this was not the point of the surgery, just a sort of beneficial by-product. However, the surgery was ultimately unsuccessful because the entire point was to make a bypass for the fluid so I didn't need a shunt anymore. But that didn't work out for me. I still need a shunt. Unfortunately, the surgery itself wasn't without consequence because I had a pretty significant stroke. Then three days later, the shunt they had put in my lumbar spine malfunctioned because the blood from a hemorrhage lodged itself into the shunt, and it ceased to work. This meant I needed a second surgery, and I was in the hospital for another five days.

I had no idea that the symptoms I was experiencing after the first surgery were attributable to a stroke. All of a sudden, I couldn't speak or move my right side. I didn't know what a stroke was or that I'd even had one. All I knew was that I was in bed, not really interested in getting up. I wasn't really talking, but that wasn't uncommon for me, especially in the hospital environment. There were storyboards in my room, with *I want, I feel, I am* written on them and then detachable words below. So essentially, I could talk without talking, but I didn't realize they were in my room. The child life specialists were trying their hardest to figure out "a way in." It was extremely frustrating, for them and for me as well. I wasn't really giving them anything to work with because I was so afraid of everything around me.

The last thing I could remember was being in bed, in severe pain, but I had absolutely no awareness of how long ago that was. It was like it happened, but I had no recollection of it, as if the time had just evaporated. This scared me; it felt as if with every question I asked I was just getting bad news, so I had unconsciously decided I wasn't going to talk anymore, because I didn't like the answers I was getting.

The stroke essentially stole my identity. Besides not being able to walk very confidently anymore, I also couldn't speak—well, I could, but it took so much more effort than you would think. It was like I was a baby trapped inside my body, except I had the thought processes of a seventeen-year-old. Suddenly my entire identity, the one intangible thing in my life I had spent the last seventeen years creating and moulding into what I wanted it to be, was gone. *How am I going to rebuild it? How am I going to start from zero when I don't even know what to do first?* It's so much more difficult when you're cognizant of trying to fix things, rather than just doing them because you don't know any different.

The months after the stroke were hard, to say the least. I was supposed to go to live-in therapy downtown, but the fact that I needed that second unexpected surgery caused me to lose my spot. And waiting would mean I would need to stay hospitalized for an unknown length of time, until there was an opening, which could have been a couple days or a couple weeks. No one could give us a straight answer. So instead, I went to day therapy.

It was hard rebuilding something that had just been building itself for seventeen years. Every time I thought, *Well, how do I do that?* My immediate thought was *I don't know*. This absolutely enveloped every part of my existence. All of a sudden, I was thinking about every second of my life and how I did things. How did I move my finger muscles when I was writing versus my arm muscles? How did I just say that thought without thinking? What muscles in my leg did I need to move in order to walk across the room? How big of a breath did I need to take to say an entire sentence? Things I can guarantee a healthy person never gives a second thought.

I doubted myself. I questioned myself. I cried myself to sleep. How was I going to rebuild my life? When you're learning how to do things as you're growing up, you never think, *Oh, I need to remember how I'm learning this, because I may lose it someday*. You don't know how to do it, so you just learn. It wasn't that I didn't have memory of my life; it was that half of my body went back to being a baby. It's easier when you're a baby because (a.) you don't know any different and (b.) both sides of your body are at equal strengths.

This was when the thought *One step at a time* came into my head. That was how I was going to rebuild what had crumbled, seemingly in front of my eyes. From then on, I just took everything one step at a time. There was no timeline for how long this was going to take. What I hadn't realized is that people are changing every day of their lives. We observe changes all around us. Life, death, the changing of seasons, plants. I was slowly beginning to understand that if I wanted things to be "the way they used to be," I needed to stop trying to "make them" the way they used to be. I had to just let them evolve. It's what I would have been doing had I not gotten sick. Everything goes through cycles. Ebbs and flows. I finally saw the beauty in just letting things happen.

Over the next eighteen years I would go through more surgeries—it just comes with the territory of hydrocephalus. There has been a lot of soul searching, a lot of rebuilding my future, and it became so much easier to change once I finally accepted that this was the way things were going to be. When I realized that my arm and leg would forever be weaker, that my brain would always need to work harder to make things make sense, it almost felt as if the shackles were finally taken off.

It wasn't until fifteen years into those eighteen years that I finally gave myself a chance to feel. To mourn what I had lost. I've never been an overly emotional person. I've always been more of an "if this is going to be the way it is, I'll figure it out and move on" type of person. I never really gave myself permission to grieve, but when I let myself feel those emotions I had pent up, it was so incredibly freeing. It was as if I was saying, yes, this happened, but your life hasn't come to a standstill. In fact, quite the opposite. You've graduated from college, held a full-time job, gone back to school for another degree, and kicked butt.

Now I'm doing better than ever. I'm staying out of the hospital more and more with every passing year. And I'm realizing my passions, one of which is to make sure no one has to go through what I did. One of the ways I am doing this is through becoming a medical researcher. As a medical researcher, I monitor studies, extract the data from the studies, and turn the information into translational data that the doctors can use.

This is so rewarding, because illnesses that were considered fatal just fifty years ago now have treatments or cures. When you think about it, the entire medical profession is research, and treatments and cures come about because of research. Even though there is not a cure for hydrocephalus yet, I am hoping that in my lifetime there will be. I've realized through working in cancer research that there are new discoveries all the time. But like everything else, it all depends on money. Unfortunately, money runs the world. But all it takes is that one company willing to invest. That one company to come up with that one test that could change everything. I used to say I don't think it will happen. But ever since I started working in the field, I've realized all it takes is that one person. That one person with the idea. That one idea.

My ultimate goal is to get into neuro research, not for my own illness but for neurodegenerative diseases. But with all that being said, I believe everything builds on itself, and who knows? Maybe I can become that one person. I've realized God doesn't make mistakes, and I can't wait to be able to fully see what He has in store for me.

Kimi is living with hydrocephalus.

Hydrocephalus is a condition in which abnormally widened (dilated) cerebral spaces in the brain (ventricles) inhibit the normal flow of cerebrospinal fluid (CSF). The cerebrospinal fluid accumulates in the skull and puts pressure on the brain tissue. An enlarged head in infants and increased cerebrospinal fluid pressure are frequent findings but are not necessary for the diagnosis of hydrocephalus. There are several different forms of hydrocephalus: communicating hydrocephalus, non-communicating hydrocephalus or obstructive hydrocephalus, internal hydrocephalus, normal pressure hydrocephalus, and benign hydrocephalus.
https://rarediseases.org/?s=hydr&rdb-search=true&post_type%5B%5D=rare-diseases&post_type%5B%5D=mondo-disease
Source: NORD

Kimi Sorensen was born in South Korea and is currently residing in Illinois. She lives with a rare disease called hydrocephalus. A medical researcher, Kimi had her first abstract published after working in research for only three months. Since then she has contributed to twelve other publications. She hopes to help find a cure for hydrocephalus. She is also actively involved in the community and wants to be a listening ear for others.

You can find Kimi on Facebook at www.facebook.com/kimi.y.sorensen and on Instagram @kim_yoon_ah89. You can also read more of her stories on her blog

Ordinary Miracles (blessingsinhydro.blogspot.com).

Chapter 8: Excited to Be Growing Old

By Andy Sinclair

I was lying on a steel table in a radiology suite in a hospital, three hours north of my city, about to undergo a transplant procedure. Sedated but aware, I tried to stay cognizant of my surroundings. There were three large-screen high-def monitors on either side of the table, and bright lights shone on me from above. A variety of staff were buzzing around. The surgeon was explaining the "tea bag" method to the doctor standing next to him. I was fighting a drowsy mind, but I wanted to learn as much as I could, so I listened in. A "tea bag" is similar to a regular IV bag but is filled with donor islet cells and a fluid that helps them stay alive and healthy during the transplant process. The surgeon then said, "Okay, folks, here we go." And the transplant was underway.

Pressure was applied to my rib cage on my right side. This gave the surgeon the best access to the portal vein, a wide, short blood vessel that carries blood to the liver. I turned my head to the left and saw what looked like a detailed black and white X-ray video on one of the huge monitors. *Is that the catheter?* I thought to myself as I observed a long, thin needle moving between two ribs, travelling towards another large vein. I even recognized the blood cells in motion. They looked like misshapen, bulbous goldfish eyeballs, floating down small rivers.

As I lay there, I remembered how quickly I had rushed to the hospital, after getting the phone call I had been waiting months for. "Your transplant is ready. How quickly can you get here?" the transplant coordinator asked. "Within four hours at most!" I exclaimed. She told me to hurry. I was way too excited to drive safely or within the speed limit. Even though the drive was only three hours, my brother was coming from work to take me. He was the perfect choice for the first shift because he was always calm under pressure. Transplantation is unique in that a care person is *required* to go through the entire process with you because of the overwhelming amount of advanced training and information involved. I would be away from home for several weeks. I did not have one dedicated family member who could take the entire time off to be with me, so my family members came up with the idea of supporting me in shifts.

Lying in the operating room I thought, *Was that only a few hours ago?* I realized I was tense, so I tried to relax by breathing deeply and focusing my attention back to the monitor. I saw the islet cells slowly and gently being squeezed from the IV-like bag until they funnelled through the catheter and into my liver. When the procedure finished, the staff rushed around me, moving the empty IV bags and clearing away the monitors. I was assisted by two nurses as I moved off the gurney onto the bed I came in on. Just as the porter wheeled me to recovery, I was told to stay lying on only my left side for another four hours without moving. After trying it uncomfortably for five minutes, that sounded like a very long time. I kept in mind this position would allow the cells time to set up a new graft in my liver, which should work as a surrogate organ to house the new donor islet cells that normally reside in the pancreas and *make insulin* . . . hopefully.

I was one of the first 220-plus patients in the world to receive an islet cell transplant, and the procedure was a success. I felt overwhelmed and blessed, like having a life's worth of birthday parties all at once. My body began to create and use its own insulin within a few weeks. This was important because I have polyglandular autoimmune syndrome type II (Schmidt syndrome), a rare autoimmune condition in which diabetes mellitus is just one of several autoimmune illnesses clustered within the same patient, me. Adrenal insufficiency and low thyroid levels are the other two main illnesses that provide the most challenges. My adrenal issues unfortunately led to insulin resistance in my body. I need to use more insulin than most, and it makes diabetes extremely hard to control.

Most people didn't understand why a transplant was necessary for me. I was becoming increasingly ill, having low blood sugars, and not feeling them come on anymore to treat them. I was just dropping unconscious to the ground, which can be fatal. Or having a seizure, or both. One Friday afternoon, my boss and I had a late meeting. Everyone else was gone for the weekend. When we finished, he left to go home while I gathered up papers and tidied the conference room. Boom! I woke up to find two paramedics tending to me from the conference room floor with an IV of high-efficiency glucose running through my veins. Thank goodness my boss had returned to ask me one further question before he left. "I came in to find you completely frozen and unresponsive, holding paper in your hand so tightly I couldn't take it away!" my stricken boss told me. I'd had a seizure.

I was so grateful he called an ambulance, but I worried for my job after that, knowing he had seen me completely vulnerable. No one likes to face how life threatening this disease can be, nor be put in a position to have to call an ambulance. Scenarios like that led me to so many other questions and worries. *How do I live alone without daily fear of not waking up? How do I explain the complexity of my illness to my friends and family without frightening them? Do I have food/glucose/sugar available to me at all times to treat a low blood sugar episode?*

Ultimately, the responsibility for managing my illnesses is mine alone. It seems nearly impossible to get it right all the time. There are too many variables that change continually. I constantly need to make decisions when managing my serious illnesses. When an islet cell transplant was presented to me as a treatment option, I needed to make some tough decisions about medications and lifestyle. How would I tolerate immunosuppressive medicines? I would need to be very careful not to expose myself to viruses and bacteria. Even having a dog presented a challenge as I was not supposed to pick up her excrement. I would need to exclude certain foods from my diet, like sushi and unpasteurized cheeses. There are risks of medical complications to my kidneys, liver, etc.

Yet the decision was easy for me. After that negative work event, knowing my life was at risk, I wanted to do whatever was necessary to allow a transplant to improve my quality of life and life expectancy. It is not a cure, but it makes daily living so much easier. The new islet cells make insulin requirements less, or obsolete, sometimes for years for most recipients. My high blood sugars and low glucose events practically evaporated, and I could sleep without fear of not waking up. Progressive long-term complications like nerve damage can be slowed as well. The better my diabetes is managed, the less my other rare diseases are impacted negatively.

I am so grateful to be one of the first people in the world to have received a successful islet cell transplant, but modern advancements have drastically improved my life in another way. My vision was also saved. I have diabetic retinopathy, which means the vessels of my eyes leak water over time and things become blurry. This is a result of adrenal problems and diabetes. To keep my vision clear, I must get needles in my eyeballs every one to three months. There, I am often the youngest person in the waiting room, as most everyone is aged sixty-five or older, while I was thirty-six when I began treatment. Each visit takes several hours and involves going through a series of tests before the actual treatment to save my vision.

On my last visit, I was called into the first exam room. The technician applied freezing drops before placing a small probe against my eyeballs to measure my eye pressures. I then performed a regular sight exam (E, A, S, P, etc.). Then more drops were applied, some of which stung. These drops dilated my pupils and included an antiseptic. I went back to the waiting area until I was called into another exam room. This one had a chair in front of a large machine. There was a chin rest and a metal band across the top, upon which I leaned my forehead. A motor brought a plate and black "goggles" towards my face. It was quite foreboding. The plate was so close to my eyes, my long eyelashes touched the glass of the "goggles" when I blinked. Staying very still, I fixed my gaze into the goggles and saw a blue cross-hatch in front of me, the peripheral area around which was night black. I stared directly at the centre of the cross-hatch as a beam ran down from the top of my visual field to the bottom. I tried not to blink. When finished, I was off to an altogether new waiting area for my turn with the specialist.

Later, in another exam room, the assistant had me sit in a large black chair, like a dental chair. It was reclined backwards, and the assistant placed more freezing and antiseptic drops in my eyes. These stung for sure, but I was expecting that. My eyes by then were dilated completely, so most things were bright and somewhat blurred. I could still make out a large eye examination machine to my left and a tray to my right with all the pre-filled syringes and more drops. The doctor had to do two injections per eye: the first injection was freezing, the second, a medication. As I sat waiting for the retinal specialist to come in, I was curious and anxious about the current state of my eyes.

When the specialist swept into the room, she first glanced at the computer screen in the corner and assessed the outcomes of the scans and other tests. She was friendly and in control. "How have you been feeling?" she asked me as she shined a very bright light into each eye. It hurt for a moment due to the intensity and brightness, but she let the eyelid fall back again quickly and the painful effects subsided. "Things have been going quite well for me lately, thanks," I replied honestly. She can often tell by looking at my retinal scans if I had been ill since my last visit. For instance, is an increase in broken vessels due to coughing or vomiting? My disclosure can help her create a treatment plan. For example, am I suffering from symptoms of an acute illness, like a virus, or has my blood pressure increased because of an exacerbation of a chronic condition? Do we need to adjust one of my medications? Does she need to communicate with any of my other specialists?

"Are you ready?" she asked, donning sterile gloves and lifting a syringe off the steel tray. "Yes," I said. I looked up at her face, then settled my gaze on the ceiling to the right of her. I stayed completely still and held my breath as a needle went into the bottom of my eyeball. Then she and I repeated the same steps for the second eye. I was grateful the freezing injections were now done. Step one completed. I chuckled to myself, reciting in my mind a quick thanks to the gods of freezing eyedrops for blessing me that day. I must keep a sense of humour about all of this to stay calm. The doctor turned out the light and walked out of the room for ten minutes while she attended to another patient. This ensured some time for the freezing injections to take effect. I closed my eyes and relaxed. When she returned, we went through the same steps, but this time, we did an injection of the actual drug that prolongs my vision for another four to twelve weeks. To distract myself, I breathed deeply and thought about what to have for lunch when this was all over. "Make sure you rest today," she instructed as she squeezed ointment in each eye. I put on my sunglasses and left with new eyedrops and a date for my next appointment.

Four needles and several hours of rest later, my vision returned to normal. My eyes remained sore and sensitive for a day or two, but I was relieved it was over again for another few weeks. The decline in my eyes is so gradual that I hardly realize it until the day after the injections, when I can suddenly make out individual leaves rustling in the trees across the street.

I feel so fortunate. I have been receiving eye treatments for fourteen years. The latest injectable medication, like I had that day, has been available (to me) for approximately seven years. The process is difficult, slightly painful, and anxiety inducing but well worth it. Because of these injections, I remain independent and able to drive. Would a woman with my conditions born twenty years earlier than me be as lucky? I think she would have been legally blind.

Like my eye treatments, medicine keeps evolving. At the time I was diagnosed with type 1 diabetes in 1989, an islet cell transplant for diabetes was a dream. Technologies are expensive and take years to develop. I like to sign up for voluntary medical trials I qualify for because improving data collection directly benefits clinicians and patients—sometimes in real time. Decisions based on such data allow people like me to live longer, healthier lives. The islet cell transplant, for example, will follow and document our progress for years. One of my specialists described it best in a recent conversation. He mused that today doctors and specialists are treating old-age health issues in people who didn't used to get old. His colleague, the pioneering developer of the islet cell transplant, is now working diligently on a new transplant that uses stem cell technology. It would eliminate the need for immunosuppressive therapy in patients, an amazing idea, especially in a post COVID-19 world when having a healthy immune system can save your life.[2]

As a teenager, I wondered if I would get old. Wanting to take advantage of whatever time was mine to experience, I have lived all across the country and enjoyed many outdoor adventures. Rock climbing, whitewater rafting, paragliding, kayaking, and canoeing all added value to my life. Volunteering has been so meaningful too. I even represented Canada at the American Diabetes Association's congress in Washington D.C. I have travelled to Europe and parts of the United States, including Hawaii. This year, I married my incredible life partner. Because of modern medical advancements, my father helped walk me down the aisle. Thanks to my eye injections, I could see the joyful expression on my husband's and loved ones' faces. Today, because of my medical team, I believe we will have a

2 1. Juvenile Diabetes Cure Alliance, "Vertex, CRISPR, and Blood-Derived Islets: Discussion with Edmonton Protocol Pioneer Dr. James Shapiro" (September 20, 2023). www.thejdca.org/publications/report-library/archived-reports/2023-reports/vertex-crispr-and-blood-derived-islets-discussion-with-edmonton-protocol-pioneer-dr-james-shapiro.html

long, exciting life together. Had I been born one generation ago, I would not be one of the lucky ones.

My family has been through so much of this journey with me, supporting and encouraging me daily. My mother experienced every high and low I've been challenged with. I sometimes wish I didn't have to burden them with concern, but I know I'm doing my absolute best, and that is all I can do. I hope my donor families feel great about their decision. Islet cells come from someone who has passed away, and sometimes the families are left to make the final decision to donate. I think of them often and believe that by living a good life and taking the best care of myself possible, I am honouring them and their loved ones.

An incredible team of people is dedicated to helping me achieve a fulfilling life. I remind myself of that each morning while I brush my dark hair, finally streaked with silver, as overwhelming feelings of gratitude wash over me. Modern technology has not only allowed me to grow older but has also afforded me a much healthier journey getting there. I cannot wait to see what happens next.

Andy is living with polyglandular autoimmune syndrome type II.

Autoimmune polyendocrine syndrome type II, also known as Schmidt syndrome, is a rare autoimmune disorder in which there is a steep drop in production of several essential hormones by the glands that secrete these hormones. Since the combination of affected glands differs from patient to patient, the signs of this disorder are diverse.

https://rarediseases.org/rare-diseases/autoimmune-polyendocrine-syndrome-type-ii/

Source: NORD

Andy Sinclair is originally from Edmonton, Alberta. She studied criminology at Simon Fraser University until a sudden illness changed her plans during her fourth and final year. Undeterred, she set out to create a career in health care and later as a document controller in the construction industry. She has had the privilege of living in eight different cities across Canada, from White Rock, British Columbia, to Montreal, Quebec, to Cape Breton Island, Nova Scotia. She highly values the strong friendships she has made from coast to coast. Currently she resides with her loving husband in Calgary, Alberta.

Andy is grateful that her fun, creative, and supportive family live relatively close by. She loves the outdoors, and lately she enjoys travelling to nearby Banff National Park and going for rides on her motorcycle. Her nickname is Tacoma, after her dream truck. Andy has volunteered for over twenty years with the Canadian Diabetes Association and more recently as a facilitator with the Alberta Healthy Living Program. She plans to continue this important work through facilitating workshops and public speaking. She believes in helping others live their best lives while managing complex health challenges. You can find her on LinkedIn: www.linkedin.com/in/andrea-sinclair-b8062989?trk=contact-info.

Chapter 9: We Are All Connected by Rare Diseases

By Maddie Gillentine

I'm from Seattle, but I attended Kalamazoo College in Kalamazoo, Michigan. One reason I went all the way to Michigan was a first-year student writing course focused on autism. The professor paired us up with local families and had us write about our experiences, which for me was the first time I'd really seen families, other than my own, affected by neurodevelopmental disorders. It was powerful to learn about other people's similar experiences and know I was not the only one. I was able to read other siblings' stories—other people whose brothers didn't live with them but with a caretaker or even in an institution, other people who have had to explain some strange idiosyncrasies. Like I do.

I grew up in Seattle in a big family. My eldest brother, Drew was profoundly autistic and fit every Kanner's autism stereotype.[3] He was non-verbal, loved spinning things, used people as tools, and did puzzles picture-side down. He was also intellectually disabled and had congenital heart disease and epilepsy, suggesting something syndromic. From day one, my family knew Drew was different, but he never received a genetic diagnosis—although if he had undergone testing, it likely would have found something. Drew lived with a

3 Leo Kanner, a child psychiatrist, originally described autism, what he called early infantile autism, in 1943. The children he described were characterized by preservation of sameness, restricted interest in activities, repetitive patterns of behaviour, and a lack of communicative use of language.

caretaker for most of his life. He passed away in 2011 in his thirties from congenital heart disease.

Will, who's nineteen months older than me, is a different story. His diagnostic odyssey looked much different from Drew's. In third grade, Will moved over to special education with an undefined learning disability, and autism screening followed shortly after. The assessment concluded that Will was, from what I've been told, "quirky." Not the most diagnostic term, but it certainly fit him! His autistic features didn't disrupt his life in a way that prompted additional testing. For example, we never thought much about his repetitive behaviours because they weren't harmful to him or others. A good snapshot is the time someone bought him a Yak Bak, which was a tiny voice recorder that could alter the speed and pitch. He'd say whatever into this Yak Bak (or make other people talk into it) and then play it back super-fast, over and over, cracking up every time. He has always been one for special interests as well, primarily buses. He memorized the entirety of the Seattle metro bus system (which was handy before Google Maps, although he likes to give the most *interesting* route rather than the most direct sometimes). But Will's quirkiness wasn't disruptive to his daily life, so no one did further searching for answers for him when he was young. Although as our family learned more about autism, we started saying he was autistic even before he had a diagnosis.

When he was twenty-three, Will was having challenges in job interviews, and he finally had in-depth cognitive and neuropsychiatric testing, which ended up diagnosing him with pervasive developmental disorder–not otherwise specified (PDD-NOS). PDD-NOS is an outdated term that was used for "autism-like but not checking all the boxes," or as some might say, "quirky." In 2013, we were the weird family that was excited *The Diagnostic and Statistical Manual of Mental Disorders, Fifth Edition* (*DSM-V*) was published, because they expanded the autism definition to include PDD-NOS. Finally, Will fit into that autistic box, which helped with receiving some services but was more important in helping him understand his identity. Now, Will takes his diagnosis very seriously, and it allows him to recognize where he struggles and why, and where he excels and why. He also is comfortable telling new people he is autistic, and this helps them understand him a little bit better. He is among the people in the autistic community who likely don't benefit much from genetic testing. He is an independent adult, and the diagnosis of autism is enough for him to get what he needs.

In college, I had the opportunity to define my own experience as an autism sibling and the feelings surrounding it while learning about the world of advocacy. This was for me just learning about the shared autism experience; autism itself is not a rare disorder (although it is a feature of many, like what affected Drew).[4] For families I work with today, many have never heard of another family impacted by the same disorder, and my own experience allows me to understand that isolation and the relief of finding your "people."

Today I wear a lot of hats: autism sister, rare disease advocate, scientist. All of these have played a role in my involvement with rare diseases. While I love all the As, Cs, Ts, and Gs of DNA, I do the research for the *people* affected by genetic disorders. Most of us are impacted by a rare disease in one way or another. Someone you know has had cancer, or has a kid on the autism spectrum, or is deaf. Many of those can be rare genetic disorders.

My career has been driven by my need to understand my brothers. I also took genetics courses in high school and college—and the genetics of neurodevelopmental disorders is very interesting and complex! So for graduate school I went to Baylor College of Medicine to get my PhD in molecular and human genetics. During my PhD, I really got to enjoy the science of defining a disorder clinically (my area of focus was 15q13.3 microdeletions and microduplications) and taking it all the way to cellular modelling in cells from patients—basically, trying to figure out what is happening molecularly to cause a particular disorder. More importantly, I continued working with people and really got to understand rare diseases.

Beyond the 15q13.3 deletion and duplication disorders, I also worked with some disorders in less official capacities. For one gene, *USP7*, I saw a post on Reddit from a parent of a newly diagnosed child and realized the gene was one my lab mate was studying. From that post and connecting to my PhD mentor, Dr. Christian Schaaf, the foundation for USP7-related diseases was formed—the founder is the dad I saw on Reddit. They had their first family meeting in our research building in Houston with only seven families. But these were seven motivated families who wanted to learn all there was to know

4 A rare disease is defined as occurring in less than two thousand people in the United States. Over 70 percent of rare diseases are genetic, and the majority have onset in childhood.

about their children's disorder. These seven families had never met another family impacted by the same disorder, and the community they developed is beautiful. While they learned, I and some other grad students hung out with the kiddos. I think it's crucial that researchers *see* the disorder they are researching (which is not always the case), because that brings a more human or emotional factor to their research. I now see many other patient advocacy groups for genetic disorders popping up and get excited by every new one, knowing they are creating a completely novel and needed community.

In my PhD, I was doing research that could potentially help a good number of people with rare diseases, as 15q13.3 deletions and duplications are relatively common in the rare disease world (about one in five thousand individuals for deletions, higher for duplications). In my post-doc, I wanted to do this on an even larger scale. To date, there are almost a thousand genes associated with neurodevelopmental disorders, and each one accounts for less than 1 percent of all patients. There's a bottleneck between identifying disease genes and understanding what variation in them causes. Lucky for me, I was doing my post-doc when we were getting a lot of data from large autism and developmental disability cohorts, so we could see what genes seemed to have more variation among these individuals. To narrow the focus in all these data, I decided to focus on gene families, or genes that are molecularly related, which was a relatively novel idea at the time.

From the broader work of identifying new candidate genes for neurodevelopmental disorders, I ended up working on the heterogeneous nuclear ribonucleoproteins (*HNRNPs*). The *HNRNPs* are a gene family of over thirty members. Several *HNRNP* genes have been implicated in neurodegenerative disorders like amyotrophic lateral sclerosis (ALS), but some had been published in association with neurodevelopmental disorders. Instead of publishing one genetic disorder, I was able to publish several related disorders in April 2021.[5] Essentially, instead of finding a diagnosis for a handful of individuals, I found a potential diagnosis for a couple hundred. It sounds small, but for rare diseases, that's pretty good! It was fascinating to uncover that multiple disorders are caused by related genes, and the closer

5 Madelyn A. Gillentine et al., "Rare Deleterious Mutations of *HNRNP* Genes Result in Shared Neurodevelopmental Disorders," *Genome Medicine*, 13(1):63 (April 19, 2021). doi: 10.1186/s13073-021-00870-6. PMID: 33874999; PMCID: PMC8056596

the genes are related, the closer the clinical presentations. Since my paper, several other HNRNP-related neurodevelopmental disorders have been published, expanding this group of disorders even further.

In November of 2022, I got an email from a neurologist and a genetic counsellor who had a patient with a variant in one of the *HNRNP* genes, *SYNCRIP* (also called *HNRNPQ*). The mom, Leila, wanted to talk to me, as I was one of the few people who had heard of this disorder. That is a common issue among rare diseases: There's too many for doctors to be familiar with all of them, so when you find someone who knows about it, it's exciting. We met up at her son Sidney's favourite place, Starbucks. Sidney has SYNCRIP/HNRNPQ-related neurodevelopmental disorder. Like most people, Sidney calls me Dr. Maddie (Gillentine is a hard name!). Leila decided she wanted to start a non-profit for this disorder, and since I knew about the disorder I should be involved.

Many monogenic disorders (disorders caused by changes in a single gene) now have their own non-profits to build community and support research, like the foundation for USP7-related diseases I mentioned earlier. We formed the HNRNP Family Foundation,[6] which focuses on supporting the needs of families impacted by HNRNP-related neurodevelopmental disorders, of which there are at least eight. This has brought together families, clinicians, and researchers from around the globe to focus on these disorders, which was exactly what I wanted out of my post-doc. Further, we've connected to other non-profits, including the Yellow Brick Road Project,[7] which focuses on HNRNPH2-related neurodevelopmental disorder, and Better Future for U,[8] which focuses on HNRNPU-related neurodevelopmental disorder; within each HNRNP-related neurodevelopmental disorder, we call everyone "siblings," and for the related disorders they are "cousins." We now have an infrastructure to give out pilot grants to researchers, to guide where the science goes so it addresses the biggest patient concerns, and to collaborate with other rare disease non-profits. This means we have opened up the door so families that previously had no diagnosis now have a whole community of parents and researchers that are working towards a common goal. There's a big difference between not knowing anyone

6 www.hnrnp.org

7 www.yellowbrickroadproject.org

8 www.bf4u.org

else with your child's disorder and belonging to a thriving community focused on getting them everything they need.

We started the foundation in January 2023, and because we really wanted to get the ball rolling, our first family meeting was that following May! Hosting a meeting based on my research was rewarding but nerve-racking—what if I was wrong and these kids were nothing alike? We had individuals with five of the HNRNP-related neurodevelopmental disorders present. At one point, a young girl and her family walked in, and she had very stereotypical features of HNRNPH2-related neurodevelopmental disorder, but upon being asked, she actually had SYNCRIP/HNRNPQ-related neurodevelopmental disorder. This only furthered our motivation to look at these genes as an entire gene family. By combining the disorders, we increased our number of patients, which attracts more researchers and clinicians. Between the families, researchers, and clinicians, I do feel like I've become part of a community, and it's very rewarding to be able to help with these families' diagnostic odysseys and their journey into understanding. While I'm an expert on paper, these families are the real experts on these disorders.

As someone whose work focuses on rare diseases and is in the autism community, I've had the opportunity to see growth in the neurodevelopmental disorders field from multiple perspectives. The expansion of the definition of autism has continued, and in parallel there has been an explosion in genetics. From the mid-2000s on, technology in DNA sequencing advanced dramatically, and we were able to study large cohorts of individuals with exome or genome sequencing. While our definition of autism was changing, we were also identifying many novel rare diseases. Now we could say someone had [insert gene here]-related syndrome, like the HNRNP-related neurodevelopmental disorders, which could include autism spectrum disorder (ASD) as a clinical feature, not as a sole diagnosis. It's unusual to meet someone who is "just autistic." There are often co-diagnoses such as developmental delay/intellectual disability, anxiety, and even physical differences. While our genetic diagnoses of autistic people have become more specific, the definition of autism has continued to grow, highlighting the differences between genetic disorders and ASD broadly.

From both my personal experience and education, I'm interested in rare disorders from a neurodevelopmental perspective. Since I got involved in research, several people in my own family have had rare disease diagnoses. Being involved with the rare disease community has provided me with a new perspective. I have always loved working with the kids, and I think I'm among the few researchers who can say that a patient (Sidney) told them they are "fabulous" at *Mario Kart*. But the parents bring so much joy and optimism to a challenging situation. While I certainly fit the nerdy scientist stereotype, knowing these kids and families makes my research even better.

Maddie is a scientist with an interest in genetic neurodevelopmental disorders. In her chapter she speaks about both HNRNPU-related neurodevelopmental disorder and SYNCRIP-related neurodevelopmental disorder.

HNRNPU-related neurodevelopmental disorder is a rare neurodevelopmental disorder (RNDD) characterized by seizures, early-onset epilepsy, low muscle tone (hypotonia), autistic features, and intellectual disability. This condition is caused by changes (variants or mutations) in the *HNRNPU* gene.

https://rarediseases.org/rare-diseases/hnrnpu-related-disorder/
Source: NORD

SYNCRIP-related neurodevelopmental disorder (SYNCRIP-RNDD) is a rare disorder characterized by developmental delay/intellectual disability, autism spectrum disorder, motor speech delay, and low muscle tone (hypotonia). This condition is caused by changes (variants) in the *SYNCRIP* gene, which is also known as the *HNRNPQ* gene.

https://rarediseases.org/rare-diseases/syncrip-related-neurodevelopmental-disorder/
Source: NORD

Dr. Maddie Gillentine is the research director at the HNRNP Family Foundation and works at Seattle Children's Hospital. Maddie is originally from Seattle but went to Kalamazoo College in Kalamazoo, Michigan, and then got her PhD in molecular and human genetics at Baylor College of Medicine in Houston, Texas. Her publications have focused on characterization of novel neurodevelopmental disorders, such as the HNRNP-related neurodevelopmental disorders. As a result of her post-doctoral research, she co-founded the HNRNP Family Foundation to help families and to advance research on the HNRNP-related neurodevelopmental disorders. Her motivation for working in neurodevelopmental disorder genetics is her two brothers, Drew and Will, who are on the autism spectrum. Maddie is passionate about helping families affected by rare genetic diseases. You can find her on LinkedIn: www.linkedin.com/in/madelyn-gillentine-699351223.

Chapter 10: Our Story Begins

By Erika Boulavsky

My journey with Huntington's disease began before I knew how to talk. My grandmother had been diagnosed and was symptomatic since my birth, meaning signs of Huntington's disease were already showing. My two sisters and I did not fully grasp what was wrong with her—she was simply just Grandma with Huntington's. That word was infrequent, but we kind of knew that was why she acted differently. Over the years, her speech became more and more difficult to understand. I felt like I learned how to speak a new language, and this was amazing to me. As a kid, I felt like I had a superpower. Many people did not understand what my grandmother was saying, but I did. I turned her disability into a magical language that was just between us. Although we knew the name of the disease that affected Grandma, we did not know it was a genetic disease and our mother had a 50 percent chance of inheriting it.

Fast-forward a few years later when I was around nine years old. I remember my mom sitting in my bed with me just after I arrived home from school. "I need to talk to you about something," she said. I remember looking past her face and into the mirror and getting an ominous feeling that something was going to change. She acknowledged that we did not keep secrets from each other and that she should be honest. "I tested positive for Huntington's disease," she said, immediately followed by, "but you don't have to worry about it because there will be a cure soon!" In the mirror, I saw tears fill my eyes while she continued talking. I was confused about what she meant. *So Mom has the same thing as Grandma? Will my mom look like Grandma one day? Does this mean I could also have this?* She asked that we keep this a secret from the rest of my family. The confusion in me began to spiral. *I thought we didn't keep secrets?* She explained that my two sisters were too young to know, and the only other people who needed to know were my father and my other grandparents. This made sense to me, and I knew I was going to make sure it stayed a secret.

As my parents were figuring out how to process this information and communicate with each other, I still felt confused and also protective. I wrote a letter to my grandparents that I never sent about keeping this secret. My parents found the letter and offered to talk a bit more about it, but it did not feel right. We all felt uncomfortable, sad, scared, and unsure of how to work through this, both individually and together. Even at such a young age, I wanted to protect my family the best I could.

As I grew up, the secret stayed within our immediate family for a few years. By the time I was a teenager, my mother had started to have difficulty maintaining a job because of the psychiatric symptoms associated with HD. She had trouble regulating her emotions, which meant major highs and major lows. There would be periods of anger followed by the silent treatment, multiple apologies, tears, and self-blame, and the cycle would repeat. Deep down, I knew it wasn't her fault. It was the disease doing this. Bottling up this secret created anger within me as well, and I would say hurtful things I didn't mean. As any rebellious teenager would, I wanted to push the limits.

One of my major memories of this occurred when I was eighteen years old and on my senior-year trip to Disney World. Many of us got lip rings because we thought this was "shocking" and "cool." I wanted to be a typical high school senior and celebrate my upcoming graduation. When I got home, my mom could not cope with it. Anger. Silent treatment. I immediately took the lip ring out. The emotional impact was tremendous. She became so depressed she did not go in to work for two weeks and lost her job. Apologies. Tears. Self-blame. We eventually moved on, but I never got a lip ring again!

Trying to accept that HD was even a part of our lives just manifested my anger. I did not think counselling would help. There were self-imploding moments where I would lose it at the hint of a disagreement and overreact during arguments with my siblings and my parents. When I started college, my mom knew it was time to get help. She decided to take control of her disease and took the initiative to build her care team. During those visits, she found the best team of professionals to support her and the right cocktail of medications. (Treating HD symptoms is not one size fits all, so it's important to find the right balance.) My mom started to feel more comfortable talking about her diagnosis, but here was the thing: We were not supposed to talk about HD. I had spent so many years protecting the "secret" of HD within my family that I did not have the understanding of how to openly discuss it.

My middle sister had started getting involved at HD conventions and speaking on panels. She brought home her excitement from opening up to this new community and showed me how rewarding it was to share her story. This helped me slowly realize that talking about HD was not a terrible thing to do. Because of this, I found the courage to take the next step in volunteering at the HDYO (Huntington's Disease Youth Organization) North American HD camp. It took just that one camp to expand my language, my understanding, and my connections beyond what I could have ever imagined. With these newly developed skills, I took another big step.

I attended an HDSA (Huntington's Disease Society of America) youth retreat in Denver with my sisters and my cousin. I reconnected with people from camp and could not shake the feeling of how well I felt I knew these people. Off to the side, a beautiful girl was signing ASL with her brother. When the board of the NYA (HDSA's National Youth Alliance) stood up front to introduce themselves, the girl I had noticed said her name was Melissa. She talked a bit about her history on the NYA Board and shared her journey with HD. She was gene negative, and she explained how difficult that result has been for her because she was dealing with survivor's guilt. I could tell she was super involved and helping to run the event, and I already felt intrigued by her. She seemed warm, kind, and incredibly outgoing. Although I didn't get to talk to her directly at the retreat, her presence left a lasting impression. My heart felt for her, and I would find myself thinking of her and her story for weeks after the retreat.

Fast-forward a few months later: I got a call from my friend from camp who was also on the NYA board asking if I would speak on a panel at an upcoming conference about being at risk for HD. I was in a "say yes to everything" period in my life, so why not? I hated public speaking, but sure—let's see where it goes. Melissa was responsible for coaching our group. We met virtually a few times before the convention in Schaumburg, Illinois.

In my mind, conferences were meant to be boring, but this was where I fully *lived*! I was entranced by the sessions, the youth and young adults I got to meet, and the legitimate fun I had. The number of friends I made who just "got it" about HD was incredible. I did not have to explain things in detail, and we all had this natural comfort with each other. There were many different tracks directed towards youth/young adults that helped me learn more about testing, family planning, and research. The panel I was speaking on, To Test or Not to Test, was about different perspectives of genetic testing.

I and the other two young adults speaking on the panel were so excited for this moment to share our stories. The convention room was entirely full. As we sat in the chairs at the front of the room, Melissa checked in on us and made sure we had water. "You can do this," she said enthusiastically. Through tears we all shared our stories. The crowd was filled with professionals mixed with those who were at risk, those who were gene positive, those who were gene negative, and caregivers—all in one room to hear three young adults grappling with their diagnosis or their choice to not know their gene status. It was incredible to see the audience truly listening and understanding our stories.

Throughout it, Melissa was right in the front row, recording us and taking pictures like a proud panel mom. She truly made me feel like the most important person in the world. She was hanging on every word. She teared up when I teared up and nodded her head with understanding. She helped give me extra strength to finish my speech, and that is something I will forever be thankful for. I felt like a weight had been lifted. I was able to share my story with a room full of people. I never could have imagined myself doing that.

During the final night of the convention, everyone lingered in the hotel lobby into the early morning hours, just spending time with each other, ordering pizza, chatting about our stories, using the rest of the time to connect, and never wanting the night to end. We were a close group, and being a part of the HD community allowed so many of us to feel like extensions of our own families. Throughout the night Melissa was sitting next to me. Of all the people, I still felt a stronger bond with her and just wanted to keep talking to her.

The next morning as we were all saying our goodbyes in the hotel lobby, Melissa sat next to me and asked me for "my digits." I immediately thought, *Who says digits?* and laughed inside. It was adorable and just how she is. But I also assumed, *It must be on a friend level, you know?* I was still coming to terms with my sexuality and figuring out who I was. *Plus, what are the odds that she would be interested?*

After that we started texting off and on, but I had so much to think about. Did I want this to become something more? Or did it feel safer to just be friends? Even if it grew into something romantic, it seemed unattainable with the distance between us. She lived in Ohio and I lived in South Carolina, a nine-hour drive away. I also hadn't talked to my family about my identity yet. Besides, I had no idea about her identity or who she dated or much about her life outside of HD. Fortunately, a friend let it slip that Melissa had dated women in the past. In a strange way it felt like a sign. I started to think more about the odds that it *could* become something more. *Maybe I should call her?* I caught her on her way home from work, and the conversation was brief. *Maybe I was wrong about the whole "sign" thing . . .* But I knew I would be seeing her soon, and maybe that would help guide my feelings in the right direction.

The next month I joined a massive group advocating in Washington, DC, for the HD Parity Act. This bill would remove barriers that HD families face when accessing Medicare benefits. We came in droves! Over two hundred people—adults and children—wore blue silk capes, with *Super Advocate* written in bright white letters, and walked many blocks together that sunny morning to talk to our government officials in Washington. We hoped this would get the attention of all the government officials and their offices, and that they would remember it when voting on this act. We opened our hearts to these strangers, shedding tears, sharing stories on repeat all day long. No one deserves to have an illness where you are deemed disabled, cannot work or actively maintain a job, and then have to wait two more years for insurance. This is still something we are trying to fight as of 2024. (So as a call to action within our story, write letters and check out what you can do to help at hdsa.org. We need everyone's help to get the bill passed.)

After our day of advocating, Melissa and many others were leaving immediately after. I offered to drive some of them to the airport since I had my car. We were all singing all the way there, and we all hugged each other goodbye. Melissa was the last to give me a hug—and it was a noticeably longer hug than the others. She said she would text me when she landed. I went out with friends that night, checking my phone often, until I received a text from her that she had landed safely. After saying goodnight, I made a small bet in my mind that if she were to text me first in the morning, it would be a sign that she was interested in me.

The next morning came and I woke up to a text alert on my phone from Melissa. It was a derpy dog meme. Nothing says forever like a strong meme game . . .

This was where we began *our* story.

Erika is from a family impacted by Huntington's disease.

Huntington's disease is a genetic, progressive, neurodegenerative disorder characterized by the gradual development of involuntary muscle movements affecting the hands, feet, face, and trunk and progressive deterioration of cognitive processes and memory (dementia). Neurologic movement abnormalities may include uncontrolled, irregular, rapid, jerky movements (chorea) and athetosis, a condition characterized by relatively slow, writhing involuntary movements. Dementia is typically associated with progressive disorientation and confusion, personality disintegration, impairment of memory control, restlessness, agitation, and other symptoms and findings. In individuals with the disorder, disease duration may range from approximately 10 years up to 25 years or more. Life-threatening complications may result from pneumonia or other infections, injuries related to falls, or other associated developments.

https://rarediseases.org/rare-diseases/huntingtons-disease/
Source: NORD

Erika Boulavsky, LMSW, LCSW, serves as the community outreach specialist for HD Reach, a non-profit that provides educational and supportive services to the Huntington's disease community. She is responsible for building relationships and education within the medical community, reducing barriers to care, and overseeing supportive programs for HD families. Erika has a BA in sociology from Coastal Carolina University and a master of social work from the University of South Carolina. She is originally from Myrtle Beach, South Carolina, and began her journey as a social worker for her local hospice agency before getting involved with HD Reach. She resides with her wife and two dogs in Raleigh, North Carolina. She met her wife within the HD community, and both have family members affected by HD. They have been long-time volunteers, board members, and speakers for various HD organizations.

Chapter 11: Two Journeys Become One

By Melissa Ryant

Trigger warning: This chapter briefly mentions suicidal ideations.

My first date with Erika was in New Orleans, on September 21, 2017. We flew in a day early for the NYA retreat and explored the city. Erika inspired me to try new things, like alligator po' boys and beignets. From there, we managed a long-distance relationship for two and half years. During this time, we were so grateful to have so many opportunities within the HD community to meet up, while also planning so many trips on our own. Being long distance strengthened a key part of our relationship: communication. I truly believe that communication is one of the strongest building blocks of any relationship. We learned how to manage expectations and to clearly state what we needed. This is going to be so important in our future together, especially because we are both impacted by HD. The only way to deal with an elephant in the room is to talk about it. We moved to Raleigh together in January 2020.

When Erika and I first met at the HDSA youth retreat in Denver, I was introducing myself to new faces and sharing the brief synopsis of my HD story. We didn't know that HD ran in our family until my mom was tested and diagnosed around age forty-six, after experiencing some of the early behavioural and cognitive symptoms for about eight years. Erika shared with me that her mom also had HD, but that her symptom onset was later in life and managed quite well with medications. Although our stories shared similar strands, they were woven differently. When I was a kid, I remember when the mood changes happened and my mom would be screaming about finding a phone number and tearing the house apart. I also remember pretending to be sick so I could stay home from school and watch soap operas while eating cookies with my mom. Sometimes she would get unusually upset if we were out of M&Ms, so we would walk to the 7-11 market on the corner to get more. Mom always said that M&Ms stood for Mommy & Melissa.

I was about eight years old when she was diagnosed. I remember feeling confused and scared, but also a sense of relief when my family told me, "Mom has Huntington's disease, and that is why she is acting like this." *Finally!* I thought. *That explains everything*. Knowing my mom had HD, I knew (or so I thought) that I would have it too. There wasn't anything that troubled me about assuming I would have HD. I was just like my mom, in every single way. I didn't want to be any different from her. It became my new normal to take care of my mom. I was cooking, cleaning up her coffee spills, and tying her shoes. All of this felt normal to me. In a way, I assumed every kid had to do this for their mom (regardless of whether they were sick). I didn't know anything different, to be honest.

Three years later, when I was about eleven years old, my mom suffered a psychiatric episode that led to her being institutionalized. I remember coming home from school and seeing the fire trucks in the driveway. They had to break down the bathroom door to get her out. My dad and his girlfriend (who later became my stepmom) stood there (I assume) contemplating how their lives would change, since my dad had to take custody of me and my brother. After leaving the hospital, my mom lived in nursing homes for about nine years. She was required to leave quite a few of them because of the severity of her psychiatric symptoms. My mom was angry that she was away from her kids and that she was living in nursing homes with no one else her age. She was suicidal and combative, and the medication didn't do much to manage the symptoms.

On February 14, 2008, my mom passed away. It was seven days after her fifty-ninth birthday. I was twenty years old at that time, and when my sister called me with the news I felt my heart shatter . . . I didn't know what life would look like without her. After some time I came to realize I had lost my mom twice: once to HD and then again when she died. I realized I never got to really know my mom because HD started taking her away from me so early in my life.

because it showed them that even though HD is in our life, we still love without conditions. We remain cautiously optimistic and hesitantly hopeful for a cure or treatment.

When February rolls around, Erika is always there for me to celebrate both my mom's birthday and the anniversary of her passing. To celebrate my mom's life, I get Entenmann's chocolate chip cookies. My mom was a chocoholic, and we constantly had cookies, Hershey bars, and M&Ms growing up. Entenmann's cookies were some of her favourites, and when I eat them, instantly I am taken back to our home on Maplegrove, sitting on our blue couch eating cookies together. Erika will search the entire city for them.

HD has taken so much from me, from us. From our ohana. I would give anything to rid the world of HD, to have my mom back, my family healthy. I am grateful that HD has also given me endless compassion. It has taught me patience. It has given me ohana. It gave me love, and it brought Erika into my life. Our wedding will take place on September 21, 2024, on our seven-year anniversary.

Erika may or may not have HD. Regardless of when or how HD presents itself in our lives, we will always need to adapt. With HD, I am always cautiously optimistic about the future. There is no clear path to show us what it will look like, especially since HD can manifest in different ways at different times. Hope has to remain our North Star, where we acknowledge that there will be struggles along the way. What is important is that we always communicate and navigate those struggles together, and I have no doubt in my mind that we will. We practise it every day.

Melissa is from a family impacted by Huntington's disease.

Huntington's disease is a genetic, progressive, neurodegenerative disorder characterized by the gradual development of involuntary muscle movements affecting the hands, feet, face, and trunk and progressive deterioration of cognitive processes and memory (dementia). Neurologic movement abnormalities may include uncontrolled, irregular, rapid, jerky movements (chorea) and athetosis, a condition characterized by relatively slow, writhing involuntary movements. Dementia is typically associated with progressive disorientation and confusion, personality disintegration, impairment of memory control, restlessness, agitation, and other symptoms and findings. In individuals with the disorder, disease duration may range

from approximately 10 years up to 25 years or more. Life-threatening complications may result from pneumonia or other infections, injuries related to falls, or other associated developments.
https://rarediseases.org/rare-diseases/huntingtons-disease/
Source: NORD

Melissa Ryant is a sign language interpreter who lives in Raleigh, North Carolina, with her wife and two dogs. She is an active member of the Huntington's community and has volunteered her time at various organizations, including HD Reach and the HDYO North American Youth Camp. She has also served on the board for the HDSA's National Youth Alliance for five years. Melissa continues to advocate for the HD community and volunteer to this day. In her spare time, she likes to train for half-marathons and explore new places with her family.

Chapter 12: Embraced by a Bond Built Beyond Sacrifice

by Halsey Blocher and Heather Halsey Dye

Heather

Making decisions for your child can sometimes be daunting. There's the run-of-the-mill choices, like should we eat mac and cheese or chicken tenders. While a big deal to a cranky toddler, no doubt, this choice will not likely alter all the days of their life henceforth. But for the parents of a child with a medical condition, sometimes the choices you face are whether or not to undergo surgery or a life-saving medical procedure. I'm sharing with you that kind of life-altering decision-making.

As a mom to my daughter, Halsey, choices were not only daunting at times but altogether life altering for the both of us. Leading up to Halsey's eighth birthday, her doctors had expressed concern about the extreme progression of scoliosis, which had remodelled her tiny spine into an S-shaped curve that flopped her rib cage over on the right side to rest at her hip as if they'd become close friends. Scoliosis is the abnormal curvature of the spine. In Halsey's case, it had been caused by extreme muscle weakness throughout her entire body.

Updates from doctors and the necessity for a decision, the kind of decision-making that alters life henceforth, was a norm for Halsey and me. Since her diagnosis of spinal muscular atrophy (SMA) as a baby, we'd been living life with a handful of options. First was the option to hold onto hope. After receiving the news of my daughter's diagnosis, I was also abruptly told by attending physicians to prepare for a short time with her, as most individuals with her condition and severity did not live past the age of three. Really, all you have at that point is hope. So the option of spinal fusion surgery to keep the S-curve rotation in my toddler-sized eight-year-old's body from crushing her lung capacity was daunting, as well as unexpected.

I prayed. Fervently. I asked God to make a way, make me feel better, make a choice.

It's hard to be positive about making the right choice when the options include a fifty-fifty chance of survival according to the medical team performing the needed procedure. The difficulty of feeling good about my decision increased when I learned that without the surgery, Halsey's organs and lungs would continue to be compressed by her curling spine because her body lacked the necessary muscle tone to lift it upward against the pressure. Halsey was aware of the situation but maybe too young yet to understand the full scope of the impending impact. She was fully reliant on me to make the right decision.

Weeks and then months into prayerfully considering the outcome of saying yes to the proposed surgery, I came to a place of peace. Peace in this kind of choice is more like letting go than being right. Making a decision usually requires a progression of certainty and a resolution of doubt to reinforce a final choice. To reach peace, however, was the act of freeing the weight of doubt from my heart and mind and knowing that applying faith in my knowledge of the presented medical evidence alongside the guiding orchestration of God's loving hand was the safest spot for Halsey to be. So we proceeded with surgery and held on to faith for a positive outcome. It was an all-day procedure that left me on the edge of my seat awaiting affirmations of a successful result. Finally, the doctors let me know that my daughter was stitched up from her tailbone to the tip of her neck, ready to heal. Within her body she now housed two titanium rods affixed with anchors and hooks to her spine to coax it into a straight position.

Together we travelled home, on a bumpy road with new pains arising from fresh incisions. Halsey had to sit up to heal, but there was immense pain for days ahead. Then there was the necessity of moving her newly positioned body to the toilet. One of life's essential tasks for all of us—bathroom breaks—became in this time like a trust-fall exercise on an unwelcome balance beam. Halsey relied on me to carry her regularly. She had confidence in my ability to lift and carry her to wherever her body wanted to go. The changes she'd experienced in her spine left her leaning for more than physical support, however. As she healed, she leaned towards me for emotional reassurance that we'd get through this tough phase and she'd be okay. She leaned to feel safe, held, and supported.

Halsey

When I underwent spinal fusion surgery at age eight to correct the scoliosis caused by SMA, everyone said it was going to be so cool to be taller. No one told me how far away the floor would suddenly become. I would learn that the hard way on my first trip to the bathroom after returning home from the hospital.

I knew exactly what our bathroom should have looked like from a seat on the toilet. There was always a certain amount of space between me and every solid object in the room, and that distance never changed—until it did. It was one thing to be taller at the hospital where I didn't know what everything had looked like before I'd magically grown while I slept. It was quite another to become a giant in my familiar home environment.

The ceiling bore down on my head, and—more alarmingly—the tile floor stared up at me from terrifyingly far below. With my eyes cast downward, I was struck by dizziness and gripped with an all-consuming fear of falling that great distance to the cold, hard floor that certainly wanted to hurt me when I landed. Cue panic attack. I'd never fallen off a toilet before, and I wasn't about to then. My brain refused to believe this, but there was no way it could happen. Mom was holding me. The straps on my back support hadn't been adjusted to my new height yet, so she was holding me like she did on every toilet that hadn't been adapted to fully support my floppy muscles. As I sobbed and shook and made my back hurt even worse, she held me upright. That was also the job of the new metal rods along my spine, but so soon after the gruelling procedure, my body didn't quite know how to leverage them for balance like it did with the now missing curves and contortions I'd previously had for as long as I could remember.

On that day and many others, Mom redirected my focus away from what scared me, calmed me down, and stopped me from becoming completely overwhelmed by the strange new reality before me. Most importantly, she kept me from falling. She would never let me fall.

Fast-forward to the age of thirteen, and we found ourselves in a similar situation. Mom was holding me on another toilet in a different home, and I was once again afraid I would fall. I don't remember what had triggered it this time, but I was panicking again. Maybe it was just sheer exhaustion from a recent hospitalization and severe illness. My health had taken such a severe nosedive that my body was now even more foreign to me than it had been after my spinal fusion. Any strength and energy I'd possessed prior to my illness completely evaded me. But it would be okay. There was no reason to try to force my body to hold itself up on its own. Mom was still there. I was safe in her arms.

Not long after this, we bought a rolling shower and toilet commode. Not all of the home care nurses who came to help us would be able to hold me like Mom did or carry me back and forth from the bathroom. This would allow people to easily wheel me there, and it would provide my body with more support.

I hated that chair. Everyone told me it was great. It would be more comfortable. It was like my own personal throne. But to me, it was just a big, blue eyesore that represented my weakness and yet another way in which my body had failed.

People with SMA tend to be small and struggle to maintain a healthy weight, but prior to my illness, I'd finally gained enough weight that I could sit on a regular toilet seat without splashing into it. Now a teenager, I no longer needed one of those booster rings that little kids use. And I was proud of that. To then fall so far that I required a whole chair to support me instead of just some extra cushion around the inner edge of the toilet seat . . . that hurt, possibly more than the floor would have.

Today I'm twenty-six, and I still have that commode. A newer model of it, anyway. It's still blue (beach bubble blue, to be exact), and I don't hate it anymore. It's one of the best pieces of medical equipment I have. It really is comfortable, and it affords me the opportunity for moments of quiet and privacy. I can shower and use the toilet without me or Mom—or anyone else—having to strain our bodies. And I've learned that it was never a representation of failure or weakness but of reliance, which isn't a bad thing. We all rely on someone or something. That just tends to look a little different in the world of SMA and rare disease.

The rolling commode is something we now pack up to take with us wherever we travel, and I balk at the mere suggestion of attempting to

general, people with SMA experience progressive weakness and atrophy of muscles involved in mobility, the ability to sit unassisted, and head control. Breathing and swallowing may also be affected in severe cases. Treatment is based on the signs and symptoms present in each person.
https://rarediseases.org/mondo-disease/spinal-muscular-atrophy/
Source: NORD

Halsey Blocher is a young woman who was diagnosed with SMA type 1 in 1999 after a blood test revealed a deletion of the survival motor neuron gene. She lives with her loving family in Fort Wayne, Indiana, and spends her free time reading, cooking, creating, and enjoying life's blessings. Halsey is passionate about her work as the columns manager at Bionews Inc. as well as volunteering with various local organizations. Writing is her lifelong dream, so she uses this gift to advocate and offer glimpses into everyday life with SMA in the hope that it will inspire readers to seek the positive in every situation. You can read more of Halsey's stories in the book *Kaleidoscope Rare Disease Stories* and in her SMA News Today column at https://smanewstoday.com/from-where-i-sit-halsey-blocher.

Heather Halsey Dye is a pastoral counsellor, resiliency coach, and clinical mental health professional; she owns Salvāre Coaching & Counseling located in Fort Wayne, Indiana. The mission of this venture is to support others on life's journey. This happens in face-to-face sessions and speaking or writing engagements to support well-being. Heather's certifications include pastoral counselling (CPPC) and resiliency coaching (CReC), and she is a licensed clinical mental health associate (LMHCA) in the state of Indiana.

While these credentials do contribute to Heather's ability to help others grow, she cites her role as a mother as providing her greatest experiential learning. She is delighted to have raised two children, a son and a daughter, both now in their twenties. While motherhood is associated with numerous joys, it can also be conjoined with loss, tough decisions, and grief. For Heather, this began when her first-born child was diagnosed with a rare neuromuscular disease called spinal muscular atrophy. This news altered her way of living and her way of thinking. Heather approaches collaboration with others from a lens of strength in adversity, like the trials she's faced head-on, with a triumphant perspective. Learn more about Heather's business at www.salvarecoachingcounseling.com.

Chapter 13: The Struggles of Being a Caregiver

By Hannah Remillard

Trigger warning: This chapter briefly mentions suicidal ideations.

It's hard to be a caregiver for a parent at any age, let alone at fourteen years old. That's how old I was when I first began taking care of my mom. I hadn't even begun high school yet but felt that my mom and I had swapped roles without even discussing it out loud. She became the child and I suddenly became the parent. What was the reason for this? Huntington's disease.

I didn't know about my mom's Huntington's disease until I was seven years old. My aunt had just passed away from the disease, so my parents felt it was time to tell my brother and me. When they first told us, I was confused and shocked, so I turned to Google later that night. I remember seeing the results and how scary it was, especially after viewing the list of symptoms my mom could potentially go through, like difficulty swallowing, chorea (involuntary muscle movements), and even memory loss. The thing that stuck out to me the most was that there was no cure or treatment. After that, I began noticing every little change in her and would make mental notes of what to keep an eye on.

During the years following the news, I started facing challenges as I tried to figure out how to juggle everything going on with my life while also taking on the role of being my mom's primary caregiver. It made growing up especially hard because I felt I could no longer relate to people my age. My main focus and worry was always about my mom's future and how rapidly she would progress.

At fourteen years old, I had the responsibility of taking care of my family's finances. My mom could no longer do it, and my dad was busy with his full-time job. I had always been really good at math, which led to me taking over. It was stressful because growing up we often went to thrift stores for our clothes and would occasionally need to use a food bank to help reduce our expenses. I felt pressured to help my mom with this stress by budgeting and following all the expenses on an Excel spreadsheet. I kept every receipt to add up what was left in the budget at the end of every month. It was a scary thing no longer having "kid" problems. Thankfully, after about a year of keeping my parents on track, I was able to hand the finances back over to my dad.

This reduced some of my worries, but unfortunately around the same time, my mom's driving began to rapidly decline. She started cutting people off on the road, hitting curbs, and having a hard time paying attention. It was uncomfortable and scary being in the car with her. I didn't know how to address it without making her upset over losing that independence. My dad, brother, and I decided it would be best to gradually stop her from driving. Once I got my driver's licence, I began slowly pushing her out from behind the wheel and into the passenger seat. Anytime she wanted to drive, I would say, "Let me drive. I need the practice." After a couple months went by where she hadn't driven or even noticed, we finally told her it was time to stop, and she was okay with it.

Since I drove everywhere, I took my mom to her neurologist appointments every six months. It was hard walking into the movement disorder clinic knowing I would need to bring up things in front of my mother about her progress that I knew would make her uncomfortable or upset. She would often look at me after I'd spoken and ask, "Really?" I would have to tell her that, yes, this was in fact happening and she was progressing more than she knew, which hurt me every time. An example of this was when I mentioned how my mom had stopped driving because it was dangerous. After that appointment, my mom became visibly upset outside of the clinic and kept yelling, "Why would you do that?" She had wanted to keep her loss of independence private from others. I needed to phone my dad in order to calm her down. My mom was at the point where she could no longer see her progression herself without someone pointing it out, and it was my responsibility to do that. I wanted to maintain our mother–daughter relationship but ultimately had to be the caregiver in these situations. I felt like I was losing another part of my mother every time we saw the neurologist.

Over time, other parts of my mom began slipping away from me; she started becoming a shell of the woman she once was. She went from having this big, bubbly personality with this gorgeous smile and a boisterous laugh to being anti-social. I remember how she used to be eager to have people over and socialize with them around our bonfire. In social settings, she began not wanting to interact with people. I was constantly asking her if she wanted to say hi to someone, and she would reply that she didn't feel like it even though she would've wanted to before her progression. This was a bit of a shell shock to me because every time she would refuse, the tiniest part of hope I was clinging to would fade away. She even began to not really socialize with me due to the medication she was on. It made me feel lonely because she used to be the person I hung out with the most and went to with all my problems. I felt like she was no longer my best friend, and I began to miss her more than words can even describe. She became a robot and would answer the same things over and over in conversations with one- or two-word answers.

The medication my mother was put on for her disease played a big part in this personality change. Before being on meds, my mom became this angry and irrational version of herself. All of her emotions were bigger and more dramatic. The anger was always directed at me or my father—it often felt emotionally abusive, although I knew deep down it wasn't her fault, that it was the disease making her behave that way. It was tough because my brother couldn't do wrong in her eyes. I became angry like her because I had been overcompensating by taking on these responsibilities, but she still favourited my brother in those situations. My mom and I would get into heated disputes over small things, and it would escalate into giant problems. There was an incident where I had walked away from my mom during a dispute to let us both cool down, but she followed me. I locked myself in the bathroom, and she went into the kitchen to grab a knife to try to unlock the door. Her mind was so irrational and filled with anger that she didn't realize how traumatizing this was to me. She was only able to calm down after having a conversation with my brother outside the door. As much as it pains me to not get to experience many of my mom's emotions anymore, I'd take that over bearing the brunt of her anger.

As my mom's progression continued, I took on other tasks she was no longer able to do like cooking, cleaning, running errands, and everything in between. People offered to help in any way they could, but at the time, my dad refused help from anyone other than my brother and me. I felt the parts of my childhood and my identity slowly slipping away from me every time a new responsibility became mine. I was constantly having to take on something new after I'd finally gotten into the routine of things. Between caring for my mom, my part-time job, and school, I had no time to take care of myself. It was isolating, and I didn't have many friends growing up because of it. I think I also just struggled with talking to peers about my problems because we couldn't relate to one another. Girls my age often had boy troubles, while I had problems surrounding caregiving and my mental health. I felt like the people around me at the time, especially my family, didn't realize how much pressure and stress were put on me during my teenage years. I could feel the grief of losing my mom in the back of my head but had no time to let it register. It felt like a heavy weight slowly crushing me.

The grief went hand in hand with my depression, which started when I began caring for my mom. I didn't notice at first because it often presented itself as anger at the world and anger at my mom for having Huntington's. The only other emotion I felt was numbness, and I had no energy left to care for myself. I began taking antidepressants and seeing many different counsellors over the years for help. The depressive episodes came in waves, and they were extremely hard to manage. The thing I struggled with the most was the simple act of taking a shower—something so small seemed more daunting than anything else. I was aware I was burning out, but nothing was helping. I put a fake smile on every day when I would go to school so that underneath it all, no one could see the broken child inside of me begging for help. All I wanted was to have my mom back, for her to hold me and tell me everything was going to be okay. I was longing for the childhood years I had lost out on with my mom.

The last straw was the downfall of my mom's hygiene. I never saw her struggle to brush her teeth, shave, or take a shower in the past. Seeing her no longer able to do these felt like the last big piece of my mom that I was clinging to was gone. I remember trying to help her with her showering, cutting her fingernails, waxing her face, and booking hair appointments to try to maintain some part of what I remember she once took pride in.

Ultimately, when I was seventeen years old, I had burnout from caregiving while juggling the rest of my life. It was May 2021, and I was talking with both a social worker at school and a mental health worker while changing my antidepressants because they weren't enough to help me cope anymore. I remember it was a Tuesday afternoon when I chatted briefly with my social worker, telling her everything was fine and that I was doing okay. I knew I was lying, but I thought that if I could just fake it, maybe it really would be okay. Looking back at that day, I don't remember driving home from school because my mental state was completely out of it until I parked in my driveway. I immediately called my social worker and just broke down. Every emotion I had been trying to hold together over the years came pouring out of me. A couple of days later, I was admitted into a mental facility to help me learn coping strategies and give myself a break from everything back home. I am extremely thankful for my social worker at the time because she was the one who got me the help I needed, and I truly don't know where I would be without her.

While in the mental facility, I realized I was doing too much and couldn't keep going the way I was. I had gotten my diagnosis of major depression and suicidal ideation while in the facility, and that meant big changes were needed in order to sustain my life. The main thing that helped while I was there was self-reflection—just getting to that point of needing help was enough for me to realize the path I was on wasn't an option anymore.

Once I got home, I sat down around our oak dining table with my mom and dad and told them that we needed some form of help because it was all too much. I had a notebook in front of me, ready to jot down any ideas of what could help. We sat there for a while talking and brainstorming together. The looks on my parents' faces were both sad and worried. I think it was because they were finally realizing how much I had been going through—it was a big wake-up call for everyone. Through our conversation, we decided to bring in outside help and got part-time home care. Someone had also brought up the idea of my father, my brother, and I taking turns hanging out with my mom on Saturdays. This allowed me to finally have the freedom to start spending time with friends without the guilt of leaving my mom by herself. I became close friends with people who were older from work because I could relate to them. They made me feel understood and supported.

This past October after I turned twenty, my mom went into a care home. She has gotten to the point where she needs a walker and needs to get her food cut up into tiny pieces to prevent her from choking. It's been a journey ever since she moved in and I'm still adjusting to it, but I'm excited that I now get to visit my mom in a place where I don't feel like she's someone I need to take care of. She can be a person I love and just want to enjoy spending time with instead of feeling like a task. I still miss the person she was and I always will, but I'm happy I can get to know the person she is now. She's happy and enjoying life with her new friends at the home and all the fun activities like bingo and card games. I love reading to her when I visit because it's something we can both enjoy. And I now have the opportunity to figure out who I am outside of being "caregiver" Hannah. I look forward to the journey ahead and hope this will give me the time to heal and grieve. I'm excited and frightened to find out who I am, and I'm grateful that this journey has made me the empathetic person I am today and shown me how valuable the people closest to me are.

Hannah is a caregiver for her mom, who is living with Huntington's disease.

Huntington's disease is a genetic, progressive, neurodegenerative disorder characterized by the gradual development of involuntary muscle movements affecting the hands, feet, face, and trunk and progressive deterioration of cognitive processes and memory (dementia). Neurologic movement abnormalities may include uncontrolled, irregular, rapid, jerky movements (chorea) and athetosis, a condition characterized by relatively slow, writhing involuntary movements. Dementia is typically associated with progressive disorientation and confusion, personality disintegration, impairment of memory control, restlessness, agitation, and other symptoms and findings. In individuals with the disorder, disease duration may range from approximately 10 years up to 25 years or more. Life-threatening complications may result from pneumonia or other infections, injuries related to falls, or other associated developments.

https://rarediseases.org/rare-diseases/huntingtons-disease/

Source: NORD

Twenty-one-year-old **Hannah Remillard** lives in Niverville, Manitoba, and has been involved in the Huntington's community for as long as she can remember.

She is currently the social media coordinator for YPAHD (Young People Affected by Huntington's Disease) and the Huntington Society of Canada's Manitoba chapter. Hannah is an educational assistant at an elementary school, working with students with special needs and disabilities. She likes to attribute her empathetic personality to caring for her mom and all the lessons her mother taught her while facing the everyday challenges of having Huntington's disease.

Chapter 14: My Unforeseen Transition from Nurse to Patient

By Jen Cueva

It was a typical Sunday family dinner. Laughter filled the air as my family gathered around the table, sharing stories of our week, the ups and downs, the little moments that brought us joy. Amid the lively conversation, I couldn't ignore the nagging symptoms plaguing me. Extreme fatigue and shortness of breath had become my unwelcome companions for the past few weeks. Still, I brushed them off, attributing them to indulging in too many treats during the holiday season. Little did I know that these seemingly innocuous signs were something much more severe.

As we chatted, I noticed my breathlessness growing more pronounced. My stepfather was sitting across from me, and I could see the concern on his face. "What's wrong?" he asked me. I tried to divert his attention by smiling, but he saw through my feeble attempt. His eyes widened as he observed the purplish-grey tinge of my lips. Then he looked under the table and told me to look at my feet, which were turning blue. And then he saw it—my rapid, pounding heartbeat visible through the fabric of my blouse. There was no hiding it anymore.

Several minutes later, my family called an ambulance. I embarked on an unforeseen journey that would steer me to the bustling emergency room of a downtown hospital. As I sat in the waiting room, my mind raced with apprehension and curiosity. Will they have any answers, or will they just get me stable enough to send me home? The thoughts swirled in my head as I watched the clock tick by, each minute feeling like an hour.

As I waited to speak with a doctor, I couldn't help but reflect on how this unexpected turn of events had disrupted my carefully planned life. We had recently purchased a new two-storey home with a pool to enjoy with family and friends. We were attending the various school activities our twelve-year-old daughter participated in, like choir and basketball. Our primary focus was family vacations and local getaways to SeaWorld and the beach.

But now, everything was put on hold as I lay there in a hospital gown, unsure of what would come next. It was beginning to frighten me. My mind wouldn't stop ruminating. It was overloaded with confused emotions that threatened to overwhelm me.

Lying in that hospital bed, surrounded by the familiar sight of bed rails and the hushed whispers of other patients, I couldn't help but reflect on my years of working in the nursing field. Nursing is something I loved and was proud of. It wasn't just a job; it was a calling. I remember starting as a nursing assistant at the local nursing homes and hospitals. It was then that I knew this was where I belonged. It was gratifying to assist my patients in managing their pain and enhancing their quality of life by ensuring they were clean and dressed appropriately. Simple acts of daily living that many of us take for granted, such as washing our face and brushing our teeth and hair, are tasks that many patients were unable to do for themselves.

Now the tables were turned and I was in the hospital. I experienced first-hand the vulnerability and uncertainty of being a patient. This was humbling and brought on a new-found perspective. Everything was different, mainly because, as a patient, I was no longer in control. This scared the hell out of me, although I attempted to stay calm so as not to upset my husband, Manny, who was at my side and already frightened. I could tell he was stressed because he was clammed up, with his arms crossed and his foot tapping the floor. He seemed more nervous than I was. Who wouldn't be frightened when their happy, caring, high-energy soulmate was in pain? He was struggling because he had no way to help me.

When the doctor entered my room, his calm and reassuring demeanour helped put me at ease a bit. He explained that I would need some testing, so I would have to be admitted to the hospital. At that, I finally became overwhelmed by my emotions and fears. I began to cry silently into my pillow. This came as a surprise to me since I considered myself a strong and resilient person, always able to handle any challenge thrown my way. Yet this all came on so quickly, and I had a weird feeling it would take a long time to figure out.

Multiple hospitalizations, numerous doctors, and countless tests later, I was finally diagnosed after several months with pulmonary arterial hypertension, a rare condition also known as PH. The disease has many symptoms, like racing heart, shortness of breath, and heart palpitations, which more common diagnoses can also cause. It took a well-educated health care provider aware of the newest findings in PH to receive a proper diagnosis. Still, the relief of having a diagnosis was mixed with the weight of the journey ahead.

I'd never even heard of PH throughout my years as a nurse. It was completely off my radar—a foreign term that terrified me when it entered my life. All I could think about was how rare it was, and as a nurse, the unknown was daunting. Desperately, I turned to online research, only to find grim statistics predicting a mere three- to five-year average life span. That little nugget of information turned my mind into a whirlwind of panic and disbelief. Endless thoughts raced through my head. *How would I continue to raise my young daughter, be a loving wife and mother, manage household chores, and still pursue my passion for nursing?* The mental and physical toll of this rare disease diagnosis was staggering, affecting not just me but my entire family.

My husband stepped up as my primary caregiver, juggling work and taking care of our daughter while also ensuring I had everything I needed. My family and friends rallied around me. They provided meals and their shoulders to cry on.

This shift in roles from caregiver to care recipient was a challenging adjustment that I still find hard today. There are moments when seeking help would undoubtedly ease my burdens, yet as someone who has always provided care, accepting it from others is often a struggle. However, I've learned that reflecting on the joy I experienced when helping others as a nurse sometimes encourages me to reach out for the support I need. I have also learned that accepting help was not a sign of weakness but a demonstration of trust and love for those around me.

At the time, it wasn't just the physical aspects of my illness that were challenging; it was also the emotional toll it took on me. The constant fear and uncertainty about my future weighed heavily on my mind. Finding an online community of those facing similar battles brought unexpected comfort on my journey. Diving into chats with the Pulmonary Hypertension Association (PHA) initially felt like stepping into another world—a place where I connected with seasoned veterans on this path. These connections blossomed into cherished friendships with individuals I now fondly call my "PHriends." Within this close-knit PHamily, we've shared laughter and tears, swapping stories, offering shoulders to lean on, and lifting each other through our darkest days. Along the way, we've faced heartbreak with the loss of members from our original crew, a solemn reminder of the fragility of life. These moments have forced me to confront my fears about mortality and ponder my readiness for whatever lies ahead.

As time has passed, my health has improved, with new treatments becoming available every few years. Plus, having a well-known PH specialist and team to help me through this has been a blessing. I made a conscious effort to pay forward the love and support that was given to me during my initial diagnosis, whether lending an ear to a friend going through a tough time or being a voice for those who aren't ready.

In 2019, my column, Worth the PHight for the website Pulmonary Hypertension News, was started, and I discovered my deep-seated passion for writing and sharing my story. Later, I found a unique way to extend my support, not in my capacity as a nurse but through the shared experience of being a patient, as a forum moderator for the PH News forum community. It's a role that allows me to connect with others on a profoundly personal level, offering a reminder that no one has to face their struggles alone. This experience often transports me back to my days in nursing school, where the fundamental lesson was to treat everyone with the same kindness and care as if they were family.

About ten years after my PH diagnosis, I was diagnosed with chronic kidney disease (CKD). My CKD was most likely caused by my years of being on high doses of diuretics to keep me out of heart failure, which is also something I was managing along with PH. It's been a difficult road managing multiple conditions.

Still today, it remains challenging when my daughter, who is now a young adult, and the rest of the family see me on my off days. There have been increasing instances where I have been in hospital and I fail to recognize my loved ones. This amnesia is often triggered by a dangerously low sodium level, which can cause seizures. Witnessing me in such a fragile state, detached from my environment and not recognizing them, is incredibly painful for them. I am deeply grateful for their constant love and support throughout this burdensome time.

Having a background in nursing offers me a deeper insight into my conditions and the complexities involved in managing my treatments. However, this knowledge doesn't make me immune to the difficult moments when maintaining a positive outlook becomes difficult. Despite these hurdles, my resilience, optimism, faith, and strong support network have anchored me.

Facing a rare disease like pulmonary hypertension presents formidable challenges, yet leading a fulfilling life is still possible. Despite the physical limitations and daily struggles, I have learned to prioritize my health and well-being while embracing the opportunities that come my way on this remarkable journey.

I have had the privilege of attending and speaking at several PH conferences, where a global community of patients, caregivers, families, and health care providers comes together. In these gatherings, we find strength in our shared experiences and hope for the future. I understand how challenging this journey can be, and I want you to know that you're not navigating it alone. Together we can foster a supportive community that uplifts and encourages one another, always with an eye towards a brighter, more hopeful horizon. It's been a transformative experience, giving me a profound purpose and passion. By raising awareness and championing the cause of those living with PH, I've realized the impact of creating positive change.

Battling an invisible illness for almost two decades has taught me resilience, empathy, and the art of adaptability. It highlights the significance of self-care and savouring simple pleasures, like feeling the sand between my toes at the beach. While PH may set some boundaries in my life, it's opened up a world of new experiences and perspectives I might never have discovered otherwise. Above all, it has significantly strengthened the bonds within my family. As we stand united against this relentless disease, our relationships have evolved, becoming our sanctuary. We have found comfort in our collective strength, fuelled by love and support. Venturing through these uncharted waters, we have uncovered the incredible power of hope, the sheer beauty of perseverance, and the indomitable strength of the human spirit.

Jen is living with pulmonary arterial hypertension, a subtype pulmonary hypertension.

Pulmonary arterial hypertension (PAH) is a rare, progressive disorder characterized by high blood pressure (hypertension) in the arteries of the lungs (pulmonary artery) for no apparent reason. Symptoms of PAH include shortness of breath (dyspnea) especially during exercise, chest pain, and fainting episodes. The exact cause of PAH is unknown and although treatable, there is no known cure for the disease. PAH usually affects women between the ages of 30 and 60. Without treatment, high blood pressure in the lungs causes the heart to work much harder, and over time, this heart muscle may weaken or fail. The progressive nature of this disease means that an individual may experience only mild symptoms at first, but will eventually require treatment and medical care to maintain a reasonable quality of life.
https://rarediseases.org/rare-diseases/pulmonary-arterial-hypertension/
Source: NORD

Jen Cueva resides with her husband and daughter in sunny San Diego, California. She enjoys simple pleasures such as beach days, riding her e-bike, and creating lasting memories with loved ones. A former nurse, Jen's life took a turn in 2005 when she was diagnosed with pulmonary hypertension (PH). Since then, she has become passionate about advocacy. Jen volunteers with the Pulmonary Hypertension Association and other non-profits, sharing her PH experiences to support others facing similar challenges. As a columnist and forum moderator for PH News, she delves into the roller coaster of PH emotions and encourages others to do the same. Additionally, Jen has contributed as a guest author to various magazines and books. For more about her journey, you can visit her on Instagram @Worth.The.PHight.

Chapter 15: A Decade of Diagnosis, Depression, and Dreams

By Kelly Kearley

From the moment our son was born we realized there were issues. The first night back from hospital, I sat up all night with him struggling to breastfeed. When the midwife visited in the morning he had jaundice, and we were rushed back in. It would be the first of many trips. He went to hospital six times in his first year for the jaundice, suspected meningitis, and bronchitis, to name a few issues. All problems that, looking back, were part of his rare genetic diagnosis, but at the time seemed unrelated.

He was a hefty baby, with a large head and low muscle tone, which impacted his development, including his ability to lift his head, crawl, and walk. As he grew, it became apparent that he had learning difficulties and was not reaching any milestones. When he turned two, we went to see a geneticist to try to get some answers. Luckily, she'd seen these symptoms once before and immediately said, "I want to test for PTEN hamartoma tumour syndrome." With over seven thousand rare diseases in the world, meeting someone who spots the symptoms and knows what to test for is like winning the lottery, although at the time, it felt more like a punch in the face.

Following the test, we continued with our lives, and eight long months later, we received a letter. I'll always remember that fateful day: February 1, 2014. It was a cold Saturday morning, and we had old friends over for coffee and a catch-up. The postman delivered a crisp white envelope with a bold red hospital stamp—I knew what it was as soon as it arrived. I put it on the kitchen counter and tried to focus on our friends and enjoy the morning. However, the time seemed to drag, the envelope was screaming "OPEN ME," and I could barely concentrate on the conversation. As soon as our friends left, I ran to the kitchen and ripped it open. My husband, completely unaware of what had arrived, couldn't understand my haste. The first line confirmed our son's gene alteration. I stopped reading after that, my eyes filling with tears. Time literally froze. All I wanted to do was hold my son tight. It is one of those flashbulb memories for me, a moment I will never forget. However, ironically, the days and weeks that followed were a complete blur.

The following month, we saw the geneticist again to go through the results. We sat in the waiting room for what seemed like an eternity. From memory everything was bleak and grey—the walls, the carpet, and the dim light in the room. On reflection, that was probably just how I was feeling, rather than the actual decor. Like a cliché, I could hear the loud ticking of the wall clock as we waited outside patiently. No one in the waiting room was speaking. It felt like everyone there was silently waiting to meet their fate. My memory of the meeting is hazy, although we went into significant detail about what the *PTEN* gene did and what this meant for our son. "It is a protein that wraps around your cells and makes them round," the geneticist explained. "If the protein has a fault in it, then cells can be different shapes that don't connect properly, causing various things in the body to go wrong and overgrow." That explained his problems as a baby that previously hadn't made sense, like his high palate and low muscle tone. I remember clearly learning that a *PTEN* gene alteration can cause multiple cancers, learning difficulties, and autism. It was too much to take in. *What does this mean for my son and all our lives ahead?* I thought to myself.

As the meeting ended, we thanked the geneticist and said goodbye. My son jumped off the chair, his tiny hand in mine, and we headed towards the door. Turning for one final farewell, I heard her say, "So, you are going to start grieving now," very calmly and matter-of-factly. I smiled awkwardly and managed to nod before we walked towards the lift, repeating the line to myself over and over. I was in total shock and wondered what she meant; I still had my son. I pushed the statement to the back of my mind and, as a busy mum, got on with my day. Although the comment was completely misplaced, and the topic of mental health could have been addressed a lot more eloquently, she was indeed right. After this meeting I slowly went numb, one day blurring into another as I just tried to survive. Nothing outside my little boy had any meaning. Everything else felt insignificant, and I had no time or energy to focus on anything going on around me.

That fateful genetics appointment was the beginning of my five-year battle with depression. After the initial shock had faded, I became angry with a situation I could not change. Angry with myself for "causing" my son's medical condition, and angry with everyone around us whose platitudes were irritating. I felt isolated and alone rather than comforted by them. Nothing helped and no one understood. I would attend coffee mornings with my new mum friends and their babies. This was meant to be my support network, where we could bumble through the early years of parenting together. Instead, I would find myself hearing comments such as "You are so lucky he is so quiet—you could take him to a restaurant" or "At least you don't have to run around after him" when he didn't hit his milestones of babbling or crawling. On one such occasion we were sitting in Costa, juggling hot coffee and toddlers on our knees, when a friend announced her devastation about her child having to wear glasses. I was so angry I could have thrown my coffee at her (obviously I wouldn't!). I felt like screaming, "Every other person wears glasses. It's no big deal! He'll survive!" as I sat there with my son who couldn't talk, could just about walk, and although had turned three, was still mentally about four months old. No one understood my turmoil and suffering. I felt alienated from people meant to be there for me; it was excruciatingly painful. My world was collapsing around me and there was only me left standing in it, with my disabled son, fighting to navigate this new landscape.

With hindsight, I know that everyone was trying their best; they felt helpless too. It was no one's fault, but that didn't change the loneliness and isolation. I questioned everything I had ever known; friendships were tested because people didn't know what to say or said the wrong thing, and close relationships became strained because family members gave false hope or didn't know how to react. I suddenly found myself in unfamiliar territory, as did everyone around me, so naturally the relationships changed. It's a situation I never asked for, and my whole being was silently screaming on the inside and trying to run away from it.

Because of the rare nature of my son's condition, finding out information was difficult. For months on end, I would spend my days (and nights) scouring the internet for doctors and information to help us. I was determined to take control of what I could of the situation. I may not be able to change my son's diagnosis, but nothing was going to stop me from giving him the best life possible. All my energy went into finding the best medical team, the best therapy, and any social service support available (e.g., respite care, a disabled parking badge, or an EHCP—an education, health and care plan). Every moment was filled with improving his quality of life. I was trying to "fix" the situation, but I was also unknowingly distracting myself from the emotional trauma I was experiencing. I searched for information and advice, I tried to find medical trials where they could replace his *PTEN* gene with mine (which is impossible), and although I'm not religious, I found myself bargaining with God; I would have given anything to fix my child. Now, it's hard to comprehend such thoughts, but it was an important part of the healing process that I needed to go through. This internal dialogue signified my desperation. On reflection, I can clearly see that not finding an answer I was happy with meant my anger and bargaining behaviour had slowly turned into depression. As the reality of my new life of caring for a disabled child set in, I detached myself from the world around me.

I mourned the loss of the child I did not have; I mourned the loss of the life he would not lead; I mourned the loss of the words he would not speak; I mourned the loss of my career and sense of self and identity; I mourned the loss of the nuclear family I thought I would have. The reality was unbearable, overwhelming, and nearly too much to face. I had always believed that if you worked hard, you could achieve anything. However, this had just "happened," and I wasn't prepared for the lack of control. I felt complete despair—I could do nothing. My life journey would become one of acceptance and I wasn't ready for that, so I lost myself completely along the way, gaining a stone (14 pounds) per year from emotional eating. I no longer wanted to live, but my son kept me going; someone had to fight for him. However, "Kelly" as a person stopped living from the moment of his diagnosis. My life didn't exist anymore. I was responsible for a severely disabled child who could never fend for himself. What I wanted wasn't important. I had much bigger things to worry about.

I needed a counsellor to help me but couldn't find anyone with knowledge of rare diseases. *There's relationship counsellors, bereavement counsellors, so why not rare disease counsellors?* I thought. Counsellors are trained to help with anything, but I wanted someone who had an understanding of my particular situation. I dipped in and out of counselling for the next few years as I tried to rebuild my life and process my grief. I began to realize how beneficial counselling was. Speaking to someone and putting my emotions into words made them lighter and gave me the ability to release them. Counselling gave me permission to feel. It helped me to understand my reactions and take back control of my emotions. My dark, negative thoughts slowly dissipated, leaving me with clarity. Eventually, I could see there was hope and so much to be grateful for.

In 2016, when our son was five, we were invited to attend the first PTEN patient day in the United Kingdom in Winchester. It was amazing! My husband and I met other patients and families affected by PTEN, which was life changing. I wouldn't wish this fate on anyone, but it was comforting to know we were not alone. At that meeting, our son's geneticist asked us to form a PTEN patient group to raise awareness about the condition. This was the beginning of the PTEN UK and Ireland Patient Group. I and seven others formed the charity to help all families in the UK and Ireland living with a *PTEN* gene mutation. In 2021, during the COVID-19 pandemic, I took on a more permanent role as charity manager to drive the charity forward and create real change. My past career in event management and my passion for helping others had finally merged with my son's diagnosis and our lives of living with PTEN. I had found my purpose.

Every year our group holds a PTEN patient day, where we come together, share our journeys, and support each other. In 2022, as the COVID-19 restrictions lifted, the patients and their caregivers spoke about living with a rare disease and its impact on their mental health, especially during lockdown. I could totally relate to the feelings discussed of isolation, overwhelm, and despair. Coming full circle and listening to these needs of the PTEN community, I was proud to be able to fundraise and deliver a PTEN-specific counselling service in 2023 in collaboration with Rareminds, the leading UK charity for people living with a rare condition. Being able to help others who have gone through similar situations has been a real milestone for me, giving meaning to the last decade. Looking back and being able to see that my journey of pain and healing has led to the creation of such a supportive PTEN community, with relevant and impactful services that are so very needed, brings relief and significance to my journey.

I am now a completely different person from the Kelly who started on this journey. I've learned to stand up for myself and my family (when trying to get the medical answers and educational support needed). I am grateful for the incredible people I have met along the way, including medical professionals, amazing carers and respite groups, other families touched by PTEN (and other rare diseases), and the dedicated people running patient groups around the world. My life is so much richer for having my son and his rare disease in it. It gives me purpose and a focus for my strengths in my career and as a rare disease mum. My son reminds me to cherish and celebrate the small things. His PTEN diagnosis makes him prone to multiple cancers, he has autism and is non-verbal, and his low muscle tone means that sometimes he needs a wheelchair. He is now twelve and is a happy and gentle soul, my silent angel. I feel blessed to be his mum. PTEN has strengthened my marriage, bonded forever by love for our vulnerable child. And my true friends and family have stuck by me and supported me through my worst days, for which I will be forever grateful, as depression is hard for everyone.

The diagnosis has ultimately given my life deep meaning and a fulfilling career helping other families touched by rare disease. As well as running the patient group, I have discovered another passion and am training to become a counsellor. My ultimate dream is to help others in this situation see beyond the diagnosis. I have learned you can live a happy, fulfilling life with a rare disease. This past decade has been a roller coaster, and I cannot wait to see what the next decade brings. You can't control the cards you are dealt, but you can control your reaction to them and how you build your life around it.

Kelly is raising a son born with PTEN hamartoma tumour syndrome.

PTEN hamartoma tumour syndrome (PHTS) is a spectrum of disorders caused by changes (variants or mutations) of the *PTEN* tumour suppressor gene in egg or sperm cells (germline). These disorders are characterized by multiple hamartomas that can affect various areas of the body. Hamartoma is a general term for a benign tumour-like malformation composed of mature cells and tissue normally found in the affected area that have grown in a disorganized manner. Individuals with a variety of clinical diagnoses who ultimately have been found to carry a germline *PTEN* variant as the underlying cause are said to have PHTS. The symptoms vary greatly

from patient to patient, even among individuals in the same family.
https://rarediseases.org/rare-diseases/pten-hamartoma-tumor-syndrome/
Source: NORD

Kelly Kearley lives in Worcestershire in the United Kingdom with her husband, two sons, and a black cat, Jigglypuff. She enjoys spending time with the family, being by the sea, weight training, and having the odd glass of wine! After graduating from Southampton University with a degree in social sciences, she pursued a fulfilling career in event management in London. In the wake of her son's PTEN diagnosis, Kelly became a full-time carer before eventually utilizing her skill set and establishing the PTEN UK and Ireland Patient Group (www.ptenuki.org) in 2017. Alongside running the patient group, she has pursued her dream to become a counsellor and help others on a similar life path. To find out more, please visit mindovermattertherapy.co.uk

Chapter 16: Finding Joy Through the Trauma

By Jenny Jones

Trigger warning: This chapter briefly mentions suicidal and homicidal ideations.

When I was nine years old, my colon needed to be removed. It was infested with polyps that were starting to turn cancerous thanks to familial adenomatous polyposis (FAP)—a hereditary colon cancer syndrome involving much more than only colon cancer.

I underwent two colonoscopies before my surgery (the first of many). The preps were a liquid diet with laxatives, but during one test, I forgot this. I wrestle with this memory, trying to untangle it from all the blocking my brain has done to protect me from medical trauma. Regardless, what occurred next left a lasting impression upon my mind and body to this day.

I was a good kid and typically followed my parents' instructions dutifully. But that gently warm day, as the hunger gnawed at my stomach, I simply forgot my diet restrictions. I grabbed a bag of potato chips and went outside to snack while sitting on the front porch's swinging bench. Not to hide what I was doing—no, I wanted to sit outside and enjoy the soft breeze while gazing upon the landscape. To this day, I still love being outside at my parents' home—it's an acreage not too far across the way from a dairy farm. My mother's large, sprawling flower beds are kept in their natural state, and in the summer, the front ditches fill with the glory of rich red and yellow from the firewheel flowers she's cultivated. From the front porch, beyond the wooded area hiding a creek, I can see the dairy farm's silo, and when the breeze hits right, it carries the scent of manure to you, sometimes gently and sometimes forcefully. But either way, it's home, and to this day, the scent of distant manure elicits fond memories.

It was here I sat, one leg tucked under me while the other dangled from that wooden swinging bench, snacking on those scrumptious chips. After a while, my memory triggered. I immediately told my mother what I'd done. She called my pediatric GI specialist, and what was to follow left me terrified of ever failing to follow instructions again.

Rescheduling wasn't an option, so a nurse had to come to the house to insert a nasogastric (NG) tube through my nose and into my stomach to remove its contents. First, she had me sit on a chair in our dining room, facing away from that beautiful landscape I so adored and had been enjoying earlier with my contraband food. Regrettably, my anatomy proved difficult, and each attempt was unbearable; she kept trying both nostrils, with me both sitting and lying down, for at least thirty minutes until it finally passed through my nasal cavity and down into my stomach. The tube was a thick, stiff plastic with a metal wire inside that torturously excoriated my nasal canal. Once successful, the nurse removed the metal wire, and I felt an agonizing pain with every centimetre of my insides being scraped as it passed through. Minuscule movements from speaking or swallowing harshly moved the tube in and out, leaving me fearfully frozen and terrified to move my head. With my stomach emptied, the rigid NG tube was removed, abrasively stripping my nasal canal again. The pain forever seared into my mind leaves me unwilling to seek treatment as an adult during an intestinal blockage, preferring to risk death than to undergo another NG tube insertion while awake.

During the surgery to remove my colon, my small intestine was brought out to my abdomen, creating a stoma that emptied stool into a bag. The intent was to later reverse this ileostomy by internally connecting my stoma to a J-pouch, a small intestine reservoir created at the anus. Two weeks after this surgery my incision became infected, and I had to go back to the hospital. My incision was reopened after I received morphine, an ineffective pain medicine for me. Completely awake, fully feeling every moment of my incision being sliced open and the new incision being flushed and packed with gauze, I was restrained while emitting a blood-curdling scream so loud and reverberant, my mother instinctually implored me to stop scaring the other children. This was my second surgery performed under not even conscious sedation.

Another two weeks later, I returned with severe abdominal pain and no stool output. An X-ray was taken, and my parents were told I was "just a whiny child" and nothing was wrong. With no improvement by morning, I returned again, and a different doctor performed a barium X-ray revealing my small intestine had wrapped around itself and surrounding organs, cutting off my blood supply. We were told I shouldn't have survived the night, a statement I took to my very core, embedded into my being from that moment on: I should be dead; I was not meant to be alive.

Part of my small intestine died from this, including my J-pouch, causing my second rare disease: short bowel syndrome. This complication resulted in three more surgeries before a year had passed and further reinforced my medical PTSD, ingraining it into the fabric of my body and mind.

Filled with rage and depression, I directed hate at myself and others I felt wronged by, particularly my parents and doctors. I became grievously shy, ashamed of my body adorned with large scars and an ileostomy. Becoming suicidal and homicidal, every night I fell asleep after hours of sobbing, wishing to die. I often required being restrained for medical procedures, a gift from my PTSD.

Refusing all help, I lived like this until I was thirteen, when I started attending The Youth Rally—a camp, where teens are led by counsellors who have the same bladder and bowel disorders, helping the campers build independence. Here, I began to find community, finally meeting peers with similar conditions, many ostomates themselves.

At fourteen, I requested mental health counselling, my rage reducing to a simmer, allowing forgiveness of my parents and pediatric GI. While my heart was melting and no longer suicidal or homicidal, I still didn't *want* to live.

In 2001 at fifteen, my ostomy was reversed. Once again I experienced life-threatening complications requiring constant efforts to keep me alive, with months of intolerable extensive and invasive medical tests. Exploratory surgery was my last option, and it revealed the issue was adhesions. After this surgery, my body slowly began to stabilize over the next five years. It was such a slow process, my mind didn't notice much of anything. It became numb to a lot of what I was experiencing except pain—that I have never become numb to. Perhaps, that was what I felt the most—terror and pain.

My ostomy reversal lit the spark of body acceptance. I was no longer afraid to show off my body, thus birthing my self-love journey, although it would remain only a fledgling for many years. I still lacked desire to live and eagerly awaited the moment I would finally be released from life.

In 2012, at twenty-seven, I found others like me online and established my advocacy platform, Life's a Polyp. Still ashamed, I remained anonymous, but when a colon cancer advocate reached out, I became emblazoned to unmask myself to the world, claiming my rare diseases. This allowed me to develop deeper connections and, over the course of time, helped me learn self-acceptance, to proudly and loudly claim my rare diseases without fear of judgment.

In 2021, at thirty-six, I wrote my medical story for a collaborative book and my first FAP children's book. Both experiences unearthed a mountain of trauma still needing processing, resulting in depression that was further compounded that year by my eighth abdominal surgery. This surgery discovered new medical conditions and launched another difficult journey to regain quality of life.

By 2022, I knew I needed counselling again, and this time I re-entered it with a fervent dedication to heal. Because my love for my parents grew so deeply after forgiving them, I lost sight of my own inner strength, which led me to believe I couldn't survive without them. The older they become, the more pressure I feel to heal my trauma.

This time, I wouldn't stop counselling when my depression lifted, and I'd incorporate other valuable therapeutic modalities; no longer would I hide from every experience, thought, or feeling that's haunted me since I was eight.

My first Reiki experience was pivotal. As I lay on a cloth-draped massage table in a dimly lit room with boho decor and surrounded by aromatic scents and calming music, the practitioner's hands hovered above my body, with occasional gentle touches here and there. She identified a blockage in the solar plexus chakra in the torso, housing one's inner power that trauma can block. How poignant. In unblocking this chakra, it truly became like a counselling session while I envisioned a swirling sunflower above me, removing black sludge that filled my torso, replacing it with the warm strength of bright sun rays. To this day, one question she asked rings in my ears:

"You don't really experience joy, do you?" "Not at all," I answered. We discussed how to start recognizing and experiencing joy through daily reflection, enjoyable activities, and gratitude.

Joy . . . that was an interesting concept to me. Later I began rolling it around in my mind. I could honestly say there were times I felt happy, but joyful? Joy wasn't something I was familiar with; when I really thought about it, I recalled only three instances: my ostomy reversal approval, its success, and periodically post-divorce.

An immense post-divorce joy etched upon my soul is one summer evening basking in the sun with a gentle breeze, looking out across my own yard and the wooded area butting up against it, hiding a creek. Just like at my parents', when the wind hits right, I too smell a distant dairy farm—a scent reminiscent of home, my childhood, and the love my parents and I share. Thinking of all these things while enjoying the view with a deep sense of satisfaction and contentment, I thought about all I had endured up to that moment. I had everything I wanted in life and loved it all. Admiring every sight and sound life was affording me in that moment, I became full of joy and gratitude.

But now, joy sounded unreachable. I've wanted to die since I was nine; I've viewed my life ever since as being repeatedly robbed of death. I was supposed to have died, more than once. I was told this when I was nine years old in that ER, and I've been reminded of it ever since. I felt death's warm, peaceful embrace during my ostomy reversal complications, and I've never stopped yearning for it again. Life's a waiting game to die, a sentence of suffering for simply being born. So what was there to be joyful about? I'd been kept on this earth against my will for almost three decades. I ignored the Reiki practitioner's suggestions. I saw no point to them; joy wasn't possible for me.

I resumed counselling in 2022, including eye movement desensitization and reprocessing (EMDR) therapy, which contends that when the brain misfiles traumatic events, it's unable to properly process the trauma and the negative self-statements we've attached to it. EMDR processing involves envisioning the event while thinking the attached negative statement and creating bilateral stimulation of the body through touch, sight, or sound, then identifying thoughts, emotions, or sensations triggered after each round. Sessions end with the same process but replacing the statement with a positive—so "Everything's my fault" becomes "I'm good enough as I am."

Through this I've learned a lot about my self-beliefs while working to untangle the web of negative self-statements I've created, replacing them and lessening my disturbance level surrounding traumatic events I experienced and future events I fear, such as losing my parents. I learned I'd never self-cared, nor did I know what it entailed. I had to literally ask what self-care looked like because I lived in survival mode for most of my life and still was at that time. In its essence, I learned two fundamental basics: (1) setting boundaries and (2) doing things that provide enjoyment and replenishment.

By 2023, I learned how to maintain self-care and began noticing joy when deeply loving the experiences I'm living in the moment, as though I'm savouring the experience at hand with gratitude for the privilege of being part of it without being overburdened by fears or anxieties.

I learned something else unexpected—I didn't fully love myself. I thought I did when I accepted my rare diseases and body. No, that was just the start of self-love. What I achieved was self-esteem, not self-worth. I still don't value my life; I still eagerly await death to take me, to give me back what I'd been cheated of years ago. Yes, I am *choosing* to live but I still don't *want* to live.

My therapist asserts my nine-year-old self desired to live, or I would have died. Though trapped and traumatized, she's kept me going all this time, denying me my one deepest wish. Immensely angry with her, I felt betrayed to my core by the part of me I viewed as the most vulnerable, that I'd been protecting with all my healing efforts. I felt gutted, and every time I hear part of me *wants* to live, that gut-punched feeling returns, anxiety taking my breath away, my chest pained. I can accept that I'm choosing to live, making the most out of life, but *wanting* to live? That sounds as unreachable to me as the suggestion to look for moments of joy did.

But as it turns out, joy wasn't unreachable. Now, I'm absolutely in love with my life, especially during joyful periods. I haven't felt this well physically or mentally in years, and even when I'm not feeling my best, I'm able to come out of depressive moods quicker.

I've learned that my difficulty recognizing my self-worth is intertwined with beliefs that I don't have inherent value because I'm not supposed to be alive, and therefore I'm not deserving of life, nor do I have the inner strength for living. These are long-standing beliefs I'm combatting that I've come to know as my reality, not recalling life before their creation; it is difficult to leave their familiarity to embrace healthier, happier beliefs.

During the course of *Positively Rare* coming to fruition, my mother's health rapidly declined and we were unable to save her. Because of my intense efforts for healing, my world didn't end with her passing in the way I thought it would. Still, although I have made great strides in my healing, I have more to do.

I'm uncertain how long it'll take to fully untangle all the intertwinements my mind created to survive and protect itself in the best ways it knew at the time. I do know, though, that I'm not giving up on myself or my healing, however long it may take. And while I still have not reached the point of *wanting* to live, I'm here for every moment of it. I'm taking back my life, refusing to return to living in survival mode only, determined to make the most out of the time I'm here on this earth—no matter whether I want to be here or not.

Jenny is living with familial adenomatous polyposis and short bowel syndrome.

Familial adenomatous polyposis (FAP) is a rare inherited cancer predisposition syndrome characterized by hundreds to thousands of precancerous colorectal polyps (adenomatous polyps). If left untreated, affected individuals inevitably develop cancer of the colon and/or rectum at a relatively young age.

https://rarediseases.org/rare-diseases/familial-adenomatous-polyposis/
Source: NORD

Short bowel syndrome is a complex disease that occurs due to the physical loss or the loss of function of a portion of the small and/or large intestine. Consequently, individuals with short bowel syndrome often have a reduced ability to absorb nutrients such as fats, carbohydrates (sugars) vitamins, minerals, trace elements, and fluids (malabsorption). The specific symptoms and severity of short bowel syndrome vary from one person to another. Diarrhea is common, often severe, and can cause dehydration, which can even be life threatening. Short bowel syndrome can lead to malnutrition, unintended weight loss, and additional symptoms due to the loss of essential vitamins and minerals.

https://rarediseases.org/rare-diseases/short-bowel-syndrome/
Source: NORD

Jenny Jones lives in Oklahoma City, Oklahoma, and is a rare disease advocate for familial adenomatous polyposis (FAP) and short bowel syndrome. Because of her medical experiences, Jenny established Life's a Polyp in 2012, with the focus of raising awareness about her rare diseases, advancing FAP research funds, and increasing patient empowerment across various platforms. Her ultimate goal in life is to help others avoid the same medical and mental health experiences she had as a child with rare diseases and to empower others in the navigation of their own chronic illnesses. She started the National Organization for Rare Disorders FAP Research Fund in 2015, to which she donates profits from the Life's a Polyp Shop and her FAP children's book: *Life's a Polyp with Zeke and Katie*. You can find Jenny at LifesaPolyp.com and across social media platforms @LifesaPolyp.

Chapter 17: An Ordinary Life with Morquio

By Jocelyn Wong

As a newborn in Hong Kong, I appeared healthy, much like other infants. Ranking as the second-largest baby at the hospital and the third child in my family, I closely resembled my unaffected sisters.

I achieved typical developmental milestones for a baby, taking my first steps at the age of one. As a spirited and energetic toddler, I revelled in running around. However, my parents observed that I had knock knees and a propensity to easily lose balance. Concerned, they sought medical advice, consulting with doctors who reassured them that knock knees are a common aspect of a child's development, often improving with age. At that time, my family never anticipated I would be the child diagnosed with a rare disease.

Despite the initial reassurance from doctors who believed nothing was wrong, my parents established a weekly tradition of taking my sisters and me on outings, hoping that regular exercise might improve the symptoms. In winter, we embarked on hiking and cycling adventures, exploring scenic trails in various national parks. As the summer season arrived, our destination transitioned to the beach for swimming, with our footprints marking every sandy shore, big or small, across Hong Kong. Engaging in these adventurous outings with my family created lasting and cherished memories.

While our activities may have appeared enviable to others, they posed significant challenges for me. The inward curvature of my knees made my legs weak and prone to quick fatigue. I often needed to be carried, and my father, misinterpreting my exhaustion as laziness, thought I was merely throwing tantrums. My mom and older sisters, unable to resist my requests, would promptly lift me without a second thought. Regrettably, my condition didn't improve; in fact, it worsened over time. Consequently, a pediatric orthopedist referred me to the children's hospital for a more extensive investigation.

After a year-long diagnostic odyssey involving numerous hospital visits, including intelligence tests, an EEG, blood tests, and X-rays, I was diagnosed with Morquio syndrome, of which knock knees is a symptom, at the age of five. The doctor's prognosis was bleak, predicting a future with short stature, wheelchair dependence by my teenage years, and a shortened life span. The doctor recommended realigning the bones in both knees through bilateral tibial osteotomy. However, the doctor's explanation lacked crucial details, leaving my parents confused. Was the surgery truly necessary, or was it optional? This uncertainty led to several postponements.

While the prospect of surgery itself was daunting, the idea of escaping the monotony of everyday life was strangely comforting. On the day the surgery was finally scheduled, I surprised everyone with my bravery. With a big smile, I waved goodbye to my parents and greeted the medical team with surprising cheerfulness as I was wheeled into the operating room. I was five years old.

During the first week of recovery, my legs were encased in long casts, exposing only the tips of my toes. Nausea kept me from eating for three days due to the effects of the medication. Humorously, my grandma remarked that I was never a big eater anyway. Timed with the Lunar New Year, my cast-covered legs became a canvas for signatures, with everyone eager to leave their marks.

In the compact living spaces of Hong Kong, using a wheelchair wasn't an option during the eight weeks in bulky leg casts. Getting around the apartment would've been tough. So I improvised. I used my office chair as my "legs," giving me stability to move around the apartment. Then, when the casts came off, the chair turned into a makeshift walker. Its swivel seat and wheels made it easy to move as my mobility got better.

Because of the progressive nature of Morquio syndrome, another round of corrective surgery was necessary as the condition worsened over time. When I was eleven, X-rays revealed knock knees and hip joint dislocation, prompting the need for another surgical intervention. After careful consideration, both my parents and I agreed to proceed with bilateral femoral derotation and bilateral tibial varus osteotomy, marking a new chapter in my medical journey. Upon waking up from surgery, I faced a new reality. In addition to the expected casts encasing both legs, I also had hardware in my thighs and pins in my lower legs. The doctors explained that my legs would be immobilized in casts again for a daunting eight weeks.

The recovery journey was not without complications. I endured another month-long hospital stay due to inflammation, during which my wound required meticulous daily cleaning. It was a gruelling period, but it also marked the beginning of rehabilitation efforts to regain strength and mobility in my legs. Each day brought its challenges but also the hope of eventual recovery and a return to normalcy. Throughout this ordeal, my legs remained steadfastly straight, a testament to the medical interventions aimed at restoring their function.

Despite my significant life challenges due to early surgeries, my parents' unwavering optimism inspired me to pursue education abroad in the United States when I was eleven. This decision not only allowed me to broaden my academic horizons but also provided a supportive environment crucial for overcoming the hurdles of living with Morquio syndrome. Residing with relatives during my time abroad created a family-oriented atmosphere that significantly contributed to my overall well-being and academic success during this pivotal chapter of my life.

Throughout my middle school years in the United States, I was surprised by my school's accommodations, which exceeded my expectations, offering a unique level of support. These adjustments included flexibility to leave classes slightly early, permission to carry a backpack, additional time for quizzes and exams, and use of an electronic dictionary. These personalized accommodations not only made my daily routine more manageable but also provided equitable opportunities in assessments. I deeply appreciated my school's commitment to inclusivity and their recognition and accommodation of the diverse needs of students like me. This type of support continued throughout my schooling.

In high school, the thoughtful measures taken to accommodate my needs left a profound impact on my daily life. From the creation of a customized stool and cushion to a dedicated school aide, these initiatives not only facilitated my routine but also contributed significantly to my achievements. As a testament to their effectiveness,

I received accolades such as the New York Times Employees Award, which covered the cost of a hearing evaluation and hearing aids, and the SEU's Genevieve A. Walsh Scholarship—a prestigious honour covering room and board for my upcoming college education.

Transitioning to college, where my stature of 100 centimetres (3 feet, 3 inches) posed unique challenges, the school went above and beyond by strategically placing stepstools to improve accessibility, even in areas like the kitchen and shower at the residence hall. This commitment to accommodation reached new heights during the redesign of my room following neck surgery, underscoring the dean's unwavering dedication to ensuring my ongoing comfort and accessibility.

For a few years I had been experiencing numbness in my hands. An MRI revealed cervical (neck) instability. Initially, the doctor dismissed the need for surgery. However, two years later, an orthopedic surgeon emphasized its urgency due to the progression of my condition, making surgery the only solution. Despite my family's opposition, I trusted my doctor's insights. His personal experience with achondroplasia, a condition often requiring cervical surgery, gave him a unique perspective. With faith in his judgment, I took a one-year break from my studies.

After the surgery, I wore a halo brace for five months (a halo brace immobilizes the neck using pins connected to a rod and chest cover). While it was initially daunting, I adjusted to its presence within days. The most challenging aspect was the uncomfortable liner under the chest cover. Coping with this discomfort, especially during the summer months, required constant air conditioning at home. However, three months after the brace was removed, I experienced significant relief. I moved back to my dorm and continued my studies the following year.

Graduation day in 2007 was not just a ceremony—it was a victory lap, the culmination of a challenging journey marked by unexpected detours. A cervical spine surgery delayed my studies, leaving me with persistent pain. A head injury triggered debilitating migraines, making every day an uphill battle, with fatigue as my constant companion. Despite these setbacks, I persevered, fuelled by an unwavering determination to earn my bachelor's degree. Graduation was not merely the receipt of a diploma; it was a tangible recognition of the knowledge I had acquired and the immense resilience I had built. It was a testament to the indomitable spirit that had carried me through every hurdle, a testament to my ability to overcome adversity and achieve my dreams.

Morquio continued to impact my life in significant ways. In 2008, I faced a new challenge: severe pain in my right hip. For someone with this condition, a hip replacement was an uncommon procedure (at the time). My petite stature and small joints added another layer of complexity. Determined to find a solution, I embarked on a comprehensive search. I consulted numerous doctors and even reached out to experts worldwide through email consultations. This meticulous research allowed me to make an informed decision. Ultimately, I placed my trust in my orthopedic surgeon for a hip replacement. The surgery itself was a success, living up to its promise of reducing my pain. It was a testament to the importance of both consulting widely and finding a doctor you feel confident in, especially when facing a unique situation like a hip replacement for Morquio syndrome.

Over the years I had the opportunity to participate in a trial for a new drug therapy that improved my joint pain and made daily living easier. After years of relying on bilateral hearing aids, I realized I needed a more effective solution. I got a cochlear implant, and conversations that were once a struggle are now effortless. I underwent corneal transplants in both eyes. The successful outcomes of these surgeries have had a profound and transformative impact on my quality of life, allowing me to fully engage in activities and experiences that were once challenging.

In 2010, through a series of events, I discovered the Morquio Group online, led by the inspiring Danette Baker, a resilient individual living with Morquio syndrome. This supportive community connects people affected by Morquio syndrome worldwide, fostering unity and empowerment. My involvement with the group led me to connect with Morquio families in China. Witnessing their struggle to access crucial medical information due to language barriers ignited a passion in me. I decided to volunteer my time translating medical documents, specifically treatment guidelines and clinical trial information. Despite Danette Baker's passing, I continue to be inspired by her advocacy work as I collaborate with other Morquio connections online and in person. Since then, my translations have helped numerous families access vital information, enabling them to make informed choices about their health care.

In 2018, fuelled by a desire to connect with others facing Morquio, I assisted my friend Maria McClellan, who also has Morquio syndrome, in organizing the Morquio Conference in Delaware. This event provided a platform for social interaction, knowledge sharing, and interaction with Morquio experts—a valuable resource for the community. The success of this event motivated us to establish Morquio Community as a 501(c)(3) non-profit organization in 2020. This official status solidified our commitment to empowering individuals affected by Morquio syndrome. We continued hosting conferences, but the pandemic presented a new challenge. Transitioning to virtual events in 2020 allowed us to reach a wider audience remotely and address various topics relevant to the Morquio community.

Growing up in a family without a medical background during an era devoid of internet access meant relying solely on doctors for health information. Being born in colonial Hong Kong gave me access to trained doctors, even if they might not have been familiar with rare conditions like Morquio syndrome.

Despite the challenges, I have learned to approach Morquio with resilience and a deep appreciation for the unique journey it has taken me on. Living with Morquio has required me to adapt and find creative ways to navigate daily life, discovering the rhythm of my body and optimizing my abilities. I have come to understand that my limitations are not obstacles but opportunities for growth and innovation.

Instead of letting Morquio limit who I am, I have chosen to focus on the things that truly matter, such as actively seeking out specialists in Morquio syndrome and persistently pursuing the best available medical care within my reach. I channel my energy into meaningful pursuits that bring me joy and purpose, finding fulfillment in every aspect of life. My journey with Morquio has been transformative, teaching me the importance of perseverance and self-acceptance and the power of human connection.

I am honoured to share my story with the world, hoping to inspire and empower individuals living with Morquio syndrome. Through my journey, I have learned first-hand that we possess incredible resilience to overcome challenges, including life-changing surgeries. I believe everyone, regardless of race, nationality, or circumstance, has the right to shape their own destiny.

Jocelyn is living with Morquio A syndrome.

Morquio syndrome is a rare genetic disorder that affects how the body breaks down certain sugars, leading to a buildup in various organs and tissues. This can cause skeletal and systemic issues, including short stature, joint problems, vision and hearing difficulties, heart valve disease, and respiratory challenges. It's noteworthy that cognitive function is usually unaffected in individuals diagnosed with Morquio syndrome. There are two main types of Morquio, A and B, each linked to a shortage of a specific enzyme needed for sugar breakdown. While there's no cure, treatments focus on managing symptoms and improving the quality of life. These may include enzyme replacement therapy, surgeries for skeletal problems, and supportive care, such as tracheal reconstruction surgery, spinal and other bone realignment surgeries, specialized medical care, and physical rehabilitation. Additionally, many individuals with Morquio rely on support tools like hearing aids, glasses, walkers, and wheelchairs in their daily lives.
Source: Written by the author of this story, Jocelyn Wong

Jocelyn Wong is a dedicated Morquio syndrome advocate and a passionate spokesperson for those affected by rare diseases. She is a co-founder of the Morquio Community and co-authored two impactful books, *Rare Disease: Rare Patients' Stories of Struggle* (BBluesky, 2011) and *Rare to See* (BBluesky, 2022).

Jocelyn has been living with Morquio A syndrome. She is deeply committed to raising awareness and providing support to families facing the challenges of rare diseases. She tirelessly advocates for the rare disease community, sharing her own experiences living with Morquio syndrome to inspire and educate others. Through her personal stories, she brings a unique and powerful perspective to the conversation, making a real difference in the lives of many families.

Chapter 18: A Man in Crisis

By Dunstan Nicol-Wilson

Trigger warning: This chapter briefly mentions suicidal ideations.

The immense pain of a crisis would subjugate me; I would lose control of my own body as destruction occurred on a cellular level, from a non-disabled independent man to a disabled, vulnerable boy. For a long time, sickle cell anemia was the beast I kept in its cage. My triggers would weaken the cage: exertion, exposure to cold weather, or stress, allowing the beast to be free. When a sickle cell crisis happened, I didn't just lose control of my bodily functions; I also lost my identity.

I was a man in crisis.

I wanted to be like everyone else. I am supposed to be strong and self-sufficient, but how can I be with this pain? I questioned who I was and how I could manage in a world designed for the non-disabled.

Sickle cell anemia predominantly affects Black people, and as a Black man, I've suffered a lot with it. My struggles have not just been because of the manifestations of pain but also because of my negative experiences with the health care system. In the United Kingdom, sickle cell is considered a rare condition, which means that coupled with racial stigma and biases, it has given some health care providers a reason to provide substandard care. The treatment I have received in the past speaks to many issues in our society. In my journey with sickle cell, critical moments in my life changed the trajectory of who I am as a person forever.

Growing up, as a child living with sickle cell, I didn't understand the condition. I knew I needed to have checkups with a pediatrician, which sometimes meant missing school. I was one of the kids who enjoyed learning and having fun with my friends. I never saw other kids missing school; nobody else even knew what sickle cell was. After playfighting in the playground after the latest *Dragon Ball Z* episode or "training" to improve my Beyblade skills, my joyous moments would turn to despair. There were a couple of times when a crisis began in class; I would feel pain that I couldn't describe, and it would always be in a different location. Moments in my life that should have been happy, like a school trip or holiday, were tainted by sickle cell crises. The other kids knew Dunstan was sick again, and I would have to be picked up by my mother.

My education on sickle cell was fast-forwarded when I started university. The excitement of being at university for the first time, in a new environment and with new responsibilities, was terrific. I enjoyed my freedom, cooking food I had tried only a couple of times in my life. I liked meeting new friends, partying with them, and listening to Afrobeats. At the start of university, I hadn't experienced any recent crises; it finally felt like I was living the life I was supposed to, as an ordinary young adult.

I had just returned from a good semester at university for winter break. I had gone to a party, and once I got home, I felt the familiar feeling of my blood cells changing shape. It starts slowly and then progresses to a crescendo of pain. Think of a hand trapped in a car door, and that door being repeatedly slammed on that hand. Imagine that happening all over your body; wherever the blood flows, a crisis can occur.

This crisis never settled in a specific region; it continued to circle all over my body, with ten out of ten pain everywhere. I feared for my life. For reference, previous crises that I could manage at home were at a level five or below and settled in a specific body region. Level six to eight, I would take the most potent medication I had at home and pray I didn't need to go into hospital. But this particular crisis escalated beyond anything I had experienced previously.

Going to the hospital was always a last resort. Many people share my sentiment, but it wasn't the inconvenience or the hospital food. I couldn't know what kind of care I would receive. I had just transitioned into adult care, where I didn't know any of the doctors, and only my pediatricians knew how to care for me. I have experienced crises in different countries and have been a lab rat because of their lack of understanding of the condition. Either I would go into the hospital and they would know how to treat me and I'd make a quick recovery, or I would be on the see-saw between life and death.

When the paramedics arrived on the scene an hour after the initial call, my condition continued to worsen. I tried my best to respond calmly to their questions because I didn't want to be labelled as angry or aggressive; my teenage years taught me hard lessons about how those in authority can perceive a Black man. My screams, my pain, and my fear could be seen as a threat. It was clear the paramedics had no idea what sickle cell was and could not empathize with the agony I was in. Thankfully, I had my mum to advocate for me and answer where I couldn't.

Finally, the paramedics decided I needed to be transported to the hospital. I had no idea what my turmoil looked like to them, but when they asked if I could walk to the ambulance, I began to cry in despair. The thought of walking in the ten out of ten pain I was in was terrifying. My heart rate increased, and I wailed out loud at this prospect. Again, my mum stepped in to calm me down and advocate for me to be lifted by stretcher into the ambulance. Once in the ambulance, I blacked out everything else as I tried to gain some mental control over the sickle cell beast, with only oxygen as my aid.

On arrival at the hospital, I was left in a cold, soulless, brightly lit room where I fluctuated between consciousness and unconsciousness because of the pain. I had a little bit of hope, as my experience of pediatric care was that if a doctor saw me, they would give me some treatment to alleviate the pain, which I had been going through for four hours at this point. Was it the same for adult care? I could see the finish line. I just needed to survive till help came.

My breathing was shallow. I couldn't find any position of comfort as the sickle cells ravaged my body. Any sudden movement led to lightning bolts of pain worse than if I'd stayed still; I was paralyzed, desperately waiting for some relief. My mother left the room continually to try to get someone to look at me. When the doctor finally arrived, they did their standard observations and questions. They decided to give me an over-the-counter drug (paracetamol, or acetaminophen) that, for an adult male, would be enough for a light headache. This decision was a slap in the face. It was like coming to the hospital with a gunshot wound and being given a tissue to help stop the bleeding. The finish line I had been holding on to drifted away. I was sinking deeper and deeper into a mental black hole; despite the brightly lit room I was in, all I saw was darkness.

The isolation, the disappointment, the despair, and the sadness all culminated into one thought. *I can't do life anymore. How can I continue to live life like this? The beast wins; I'm tired of fighting.* I then held my breath as a sign of resignation. At least in death, I wouldn't have the torment of pain like this.

Then, in my lowest depths, the light came through, and God brought into my mind the people who keep saving me when I am in a crisis. Despite this pain, despite isolating myself, there were still people who cared for me. My faith teaches me that when humanity abandons you, there is still a presence that never will, and it was at that moment I felt that presence. God told me this pain would pass, and I still have a purpose. I was able to hold on until I was finally given the proper treatment and care.

In my recovery, I promised myself and God that I would never get to that point in my life again where I was so low and so defeated. I blamed the hospital for this and swore off going to the hospital altogether because of the initial care I received. What became my promise turned into my mental curse, as I spent each day counting my time out of the hospital. During this period, I experienced crises that were eight out of ten, which on my pain scale meant I should go into hospital. However, with what I experienced and for the sake of my streak, I suffered at home instead. It was better to have my fate in my own hands than to leave it to the doctors trained to help me. I developed hazardous behaviours; I overdosed on medication to control my pain at home instead. I did reckless things like that for six years to avoid the hospital and maintain a streak I was desperate to keep.

I did my best to keep the beast in its cage, but little did I know that it kept me locked up. My cage kept me isolated from my friends and family because I felt like I couldn't share what I was going through with sickle cell. It was easier to suffer alone than to be a burden on anyone else; after all, nobody would understand what I was going through. The joys of being a young adult passed me by because the fears from my childhood of excitement equalling pain lingered. It was easier not to be hopeful for things than to be disappointed by a crisis.

Society had told me that to be a man, I was supposed to be strong in all areas of my life. Sickle cell was the only area I wasn't, so that had to be hidden. I was becoming a man without the fullness of who I was because I severed my identity. I was Dunstan without sickle cell to the world, but in the quietness and isolation of my room in crisis, it was the beast that emerged. For six years, I was a man in crisis because even after the pain had gone, the mental scars were still present as the isolation continued.

Eventually, in 2018, my six-year streak of avoiding a hospital admission ended when I was experiencing another ten out of ten crisis. I didn't reach the same depths of where I wanted to unalive myself, but I was left mentally distraught. At this point, I had my first career job and was already in a hospital. How was I supposed to do this? How was I supposed to provide for and support my family with such a chronic condition? I was supposed to be the strong one supporting my mum and brother, and yet, in this moment, I was weak and helpless. I mourned what my life could have looked like.

My mother played an instrumental role in recommending therapy to me. I was sure she would tell me to pray, which would have ended the conversation. However, her encouragement to seek help began my journey to healing. Therapy was not what I expected; I didn't recognize the various ways sickle cell had impacted me until my counselling sessions. My only comfort zone was myself, which meant my priority was self-preservation when difficult moments occurred in relationships with others. It was easier to avoid problems and conflict than to address them head-on. My genetic condition is invisible, and so it made it easier to hide from everyone and be accepted into society. I was already struggling to fit in as a young Black man, let alone a young Black man with a chronic condition. To break out of what I had always known—the isolation, the fear, the self-preservation—my therapist advised me to speak about my experiences with the world.

Therapy and my support network pushed me out of my hesitancy and shyness. The journey was a slow burner, a podcast here and there or a post about something I did on social media. I was scared to be so vulnerable and mentally and physically drained from the initial experiences of sharing. From keeping everything locked to being open, I'd dramatically shifted what I had always done. It started as a self-development tool to grow mentally, physically, and spiritually stronger, but my advocacy went beyond that, as I connected with other patients with sickle cell to help share their struggles and amplify their voices. I realized there were thousands of people living with this disease who, like me, were not speaking out about how it impacts them because of fear and shame.

Today looks very different; my personal development from therapy and sharing my stories has drastically improved my mental well-being compared with what I went through before 2018. I've found purpose and strength in being vulnerable while giving myself grace when I sometimes fall ill. I could not tell you the last time I was in hospital with a crisis. That's not to say I haven't been to the hospital since 2018, but I don't keep track. I've freed myself from the ticking time bomb of a hospital admission and now focus more on the present. I've learned a lot about my body during this time, and adopting a more holistic approach to how I look after myself has led to many health benefits. I've been able to identify the type of man I am. I am mentally stronger, physically growing, and grounded in the fact that my path will look different from other people's, and that's okay.

I've escaped the shackles of my cage and can confidently say I'm being true to myself. Sickle cell doesn't have a cage either; I walk with it, learning to control it rather than hide and fear it. Finding peace with myself has led me to combine the two identities I had for so long into one. I am Dunstan, and I have sickle cell; I am no longer a man in crisis.

Dunstan is living with sickle cell disease.

Sickle cell disease (SCD) is characterized by the presence of sickle, or crescent-shaped, red blood cells (erythrocytes) in the bloodstream. These crescent-shaped cells are stiff and sticky and interact with other cells and the blood clotting system to block blood flow in the very tiny blood vessels (capillaries) of the peripheral blood system (blood vessels outside of the heart). This prevents the normal flow of nutrition and oxygen (as red blood cells are responsible for carrying oxygen throughout the body). Common symptoms associated with SCD include excruciating bone pain, chest pain, severe infections (primarily in children), low levels of circulating red blood cells (anemia) and yellowing of the skin (jaundice). The blocked blood flow can also cause severe organ damage including stroke.

https://rarediseases.org/rare-diseases/sickle-cell-disease/

Source: NORD

Dunstan Nicol-Wilson is from South East London, United Kingdom. He works as a project manager and has a master's degree in public health with a global health focus. Dunstan was diagnosed with the "invisible disorder," sickle cell disease, from birth. He advocates for the condition as a mentor, freelance writer, and speaker. Through his advocacy, he aims to raise awareness for sickle cell, encourage others to share their stories, and showcase all the ups and downs of living with the condition. Dunstan loves travelling, anime, food, and Manchester United.

Chapter 19: I Am a RAREsie Warrior

By Joanne Paquette

I was born in December 1963, the first girl and the last child in my family. At birth, my feet were bent the wrong way and my legs were out of shape. After a few months with no change, my parents knew something had to be done. Both of my legs were put into casts when I was six months old, with the goal of shaping the young bones in the proper direction. After six weeks, the casts were removed, and X-rays revealed some improvement. However, to ensure the bones would continue to develop in the proper direction, the physician requested a brace be made for my feet—white baby booties with a metal bar attached to the soles, toes pointed outward. My mom would put my feet into the baby shoes at night and place me on my tummy. After a few months, the physician had no more concerns about my legs, and the night brace was no longer needed.

About a year and a half later, once I had started walking, my dad noticed that my right leg was growing outward. I had a limp, and my femur was deformed—it was bowing. My mom was in complete disbelief that this was happening to me. When I was three and a half years old, my legs and ankles started causing me a lot of pain. Finally, my parents sought the help of a cousin who had recently graduated from medical school as an orthopaedic surgeon, Dr. Denis Desjardins.

Once we met with Denis (he preferred I call him by his first name), X-rays revealed enchondromas (tumours) in my right upper distal femur, both lower extremities, and two toes in my right foot. Denis had a strong suspicion of multiple enchondromatosis: tumours in the cartilage (a.k.a. Ollier disease). The tumours were mostly on the right side of my body, which was noted to be a distinction in females, and with the little information we had, this was helpful. Denis suggested I see a doctor at SickKids in Toronto to confirm his diagnosis. This doctor told my parents that the ratio for this disease was one in a million, and I was that ONE.

Because of a lack of information, complete amputation of my right leg was proposed, but my mother opposed it. We did not want to move to Toronto, nor did I wish to continue seeing the doctor at SickKids. I knew I wanted Denis to be my doctor—even as a child, I somehow knew I could trust him. He was calm, he never rushed when he spoke with me, and he would often whistle as he approached my hospital room. I still hear him to this day. Denis explained how a positive attitude was best; he described some mumbo jumbo medical terms to my parents, but to me, it meant nothing, really. My parents were content and very hopeful, and therefore I was too! Denis chose to devote his time and energy to my surgical procedures. He had never performed surgery on someone with Ollier disease, with enchondromas; there was no prior research on file in Canada or in the United States at the time.

I didn't know what to expect. I had just turned five years old in December. I remember being excited and thought I was going to some sort of a hotel. Looking back now, it makes me laugh. The windows had bars on them, I had to wear their red and white pajamas, and visiting hours were strictly enforced. The food was what you got—no outside food was allowed. I don't remember much else except running up and down the hallway with a male patient, my age, the night before my surgery. Either the hallway lights were out or the halls were gloomy. The place itself looked old and scary, especially with nuns in charge. They were strict and mean too. It was by no means a hospital for kids!

Recently I have been trying to read the contents of my medical records, googling the big words and reflecting on how much I experienced. When Denis retired, he had given me all my files and X-rays, which he had in his downtown office. One of the most important pieces of paper is his description of my diagnosis, in his own handwriting. I also have the typed yellow-copy transcript from my first surgery, dated January 19, 1969:

"An incision was made at the distal ⅓ of the thigh deepened through the subcutaneous tissue and opening the inverting fascia, the intermuscular septum between the vastus lateralis and the biceps muscle was approached and the femoral shaft was exposed . . . Then from the bone bank we selected a piece of bone . . . The subcutaneous tissue was closed using plain catgut."

Once I was brought to my hospital room from recovery, my mom was waiting for me. I had a body cast, a long needle in my femur to drain the blood coming out of my cast into a Hemovac bag, and IVs in both hands. My mother was not prepared to see me this way (nor do I believe Denis knew he would put me in a body cast), and she started to cry. She told me I hugged her and said I was just fine, it would all be okay. My mom knew from that moment she had a spunky fighter, as she called me, on her hands.

I would be at the local hospital for two weeks. My life changed from that day and helped shape me into the person I am today. Being alone in a room away from my own bedroom, in a bed I could not get out of, encouraged me to develop other skills: how to distinguish people by their walk in the hallway, smells, and schedules. Independence came at a young age, and to this day I remain independent, strong, and determined. Denis saw this in me, and he encouraged it. After I recovered, he was careful about what sports I could take part in; however, he believed I should try, and that I deserved to.

As months passed by, it was noted that my femur was starting to bow more, and the lower part of my leg was bowing out to the side again. This was causing me severe pain. Denis suggested another surgery. He told my parents this type of surgery would most likely be required every year (at one point it became every nine months) and most likely would continue until my growth spurt was done. This was due to the enchondromas (tumours) in my femur constantly appearing or growing. Although femoral bone grafts were being performed on me, only a certain number could be grafted and replaced with bone from the bone bank. My bones were younger than most bones available in the bone bank, and Denis focused on the prominent enchondromas (tumours). Scoliosis had also started to develop.

You need to remember that Denis had no references, no information, nothing to really guide him, because Ollier disease was so rare. He even travelled abroad to learn more so he could treat me better. Denis will always hold a place in my heart, and I miss him dearly. He was an amazing doctor and a remarkable person.

In between surgeries I often fractured a bone, usually my femur. I have fractured my fingers, wrists, forearms, legs (tibia, fibula, femur), toes, ankles, feet, pelvis, right patella, ribs . . . I think that's it! The disease causes the tumours to eat away at the cartilage, trying to manifest through to the bone, therefore causing a delay in growth and development. As I stated already, my right lower leg would continue to grow outward, and this caused a lot of pain, especially between five and eleven years old, but it was something I just had to adapt to.

As an adult, it took me some time to divide and sort all my medical files from various hospitals. I've had so many surgeries in my life that I cannot simply list them in chronological order. So much has happened it is hard to get things straight, but here are a few more key memories that stand out for me.

At one point I had two surgeries three days apart and both my legs in casts at the same time! My right leg was 6.5 centimetres shorter than my left. The first surgery was done on my left leg. The two growth plates were blocked, to prevent my left leg from growing more, with hope that the right leg would catch up, but that did not happen. The second surgery was on my right femur, the same procedure as always: osteotomy and bone grafts with bone from the bone bank. Jumping forward several years, I fractured both wrists at the same time. Having both wrists and forearms in casts at the same time was horrible. If you asked which I preferred, it was both legs in a cast at the same time.

Another time I was in the hospital for three months. During that time I had an external fixator known as the Wagner device; two rods were drilled into my lower right leg bones, two more a little lower than knee level. The fixator was placed onto the rods on the inner part of my right leg. It had a dial at the top that I had to turn halfway, once per day. On one particular day, I was in more pain than usual. I kept buzzing for a nurse, and one did come see me. She saw nothing and thought I was just complaining. I kept buzzing for the nurses, as I felt worse. They chose to ignore me. My parents arrived for a visit to find me covered in my own blood. I had turned the dial a little too much, causing the wound around the rods to open. I remember the moment clearly, the heat of the blood on my chest, the concern on my mother's face, and how very weak I was. The nurse was rushing around, trying to get the blood bag line hooked up to my IV. I required two blood transfusions. Had my parents not shown up, I would have died. Years later I found out that those blood transfusions infected me with hepatitis C.

After all that, you can well imagine why I started drinking when I was twelve years old. Booze was my getaway. I even got caught drinking beer with another patient when I had my leg-lengthening procedure. I met another girl and we hit it off. She was discharged but returned two weeks later and brought six beers with her. Yes, six beers! She put me in a wheelchair, and we went one floor down to the wheelchair bathroom. We drank the beers in about forty-five minutes, then put the empties in the garbage bin. The next day, the head nurse called us into her office and pulled the empty beer bottles from a bag.

One of my worst memories was when I fractured my right femur, again. This time it was a compound fracture, and my bone tore through my flesh. We resided in Quebec at the time, and I was in the local hospital, run by nuns. The orthopaedic team had never heard of Ollier disease and had no clue what to do with me. They consulted with Denis in Ottawa—I am very grateful for that. He explained my situation to the medical team and concluded that surgery was required to put my right leg in traction. Although my family is bilingual, French and English, the province of Quebec at the time (1972) was very separatist. It was the time of the FLQ and a time of division and great unrest in the province. The nuns did not allow me to speak English in their presence. I was ignored, was treated unfairly, and developed a very bad case of bedsores. I was in traction for three months. I could not leave my bed or the hospital room.

I have been through so much, and yet, at times I think I complain for no reason. Reading all the medical records and the notes about all that happened to me is overwhelming, and I have many more files to read. I am glad to have these files, and proud to be able to look back at who I was and how far I have come.

Throughout my life, the other big issue was that we were alone in all this, aside from Denis, of course. We knew of nobody else with the disease, and I didn't have anyone to guide me regarding the outcome. My parents were constantly facing huge life-changing decisions for me. I became a guinea pig, and this is something I am proud of. The surgical procedures that were tried on me are now being conducted on others with the disease.

Now I am sixty years old, and my body is deteriorating. I fear for my future and how the cost of living is affecting everyone, but especially the disabled RAREsie community. The federal government promised funding for the rare disease community, for desperately needed medication and devices. The costs for such things are too expensive for many families. Children are losing their lives due to this lack of funding. The federal government established the Canada Disability Benefit, which was supposed to get disabled people out of poverty, then announced a mere $2,400 per year. I also believe that if you qualify for a Canada Pension Plan Disability Benefit, you should keep it, no clawbacks. Although I am very proud to be Canadian, the government fails the disabled and rare disease community in so many ways that I feel bad for families, including my own. I am doing what I can to make a difference.

I hope to create change and opportunity with the RAREsies Rule Ollier Educational Scholarship Program. The scholarships will help secure the future of an Ollier RAREsie and bring some peace of mind to their parents. I don't care about your grades—I care that you need a secure future. Learning is a great thing!

I have *always* wanted to meet someone else with the disease, and I finally found others! It was a day I will never forget. I had typed "multiple enchondromatosis" into the Facebook search engine and *wow*! There was a support group in the United Kingdom. So I decided to create my own here in Canada. The one-person support group I founded began to grow. And now there are 110 people in the group. Support, guidance, understanding, and acceptance are all part of the process—this is what I hope I provide to the RAREsies Rule group members. The ratio for the disease is now one in 100,000. I was alone for years, and to some degree I still am because I have yet to meet an Ollier RAREsie Warrior in person.

I have had a tough life. However, I love to smile, I love to laugh, and mostly I love my family. I have three amazing children: Jason, Ashlee (her husband Adam is the best), and Gavin. My granddaughters, Peyton and Everleigh, make my world complete. My love for them is unconditional and forever. My family, my children, are my everything, and I can proudly say I raised them well. They are the greatest joy in my life.

To all those RAREsie Warriors out there, this is my wish to you: May you find joy in your endeavours. Stay strong, Warriors! We are certainly a different kind, but the best kind. RAREsies are proud, determined, and strong, and we truly never give up. Do not let anyone make you think otherwise. You may get knocked down, but you will get up again!

Falling is just a trip in your day.
Getting back up is the peak.

Joanne is living with Ollier disease.

Ollier disease is a rare skeletal disorder characterized by abnormal bone development (skeletal dysplasia). While this disorder may be present at birth (congenital), it may not become apparent until early childhood when symptoms such as deformities or improper limb growth are more obvious. Ollier disease manifests as greater than normal growth of the cartilage in the long bones of the legs and arms so that growth is abnormal and the outer layer of the bone becomes thin and more fragile. These masses of cartilage are benign (non-cancerous) tumours known as enchondromas. Enchondromas may occur at any time. In about 30 percent of patients, the enchondromas may undergo malignant changes to a cancer such as chondrosarcomas.
https://rarediseases.org/rare-diseases/ollier-disease/
Source: NORD

Joanne Paquette is a dedicated advocate and founder of RAREsies Rule/Ollier's Disease Canada. Driven by her perseverance and selflessness, known for her empathy and compassion, she is always ready to support those around her. Joanne has a contagious smile that brightens any room. Her joyful spirit is evident in her love of making others laugh, spreading positivity wherever she goes.

Chapter 20: Finding Sunrise

By Kerri Mauer

Long before the sun rose on that brisk October morning, I got dressed, packed my lunch, and headed to work. I was wired from steroids and tired of tossing and turning, so I dragged my weak body out of bed. The only car in the lot at 5:00 a.m. was one of a senior colleague I admired deeply, and because I was feeling such despair, I considered it a sign and made my way to Kristin's room.

She sat hunched over her desk, grading papers by the light of one small desk lamp. Our conversation quickly turned from our day's lessons to the stress of the job. Although my health limitations were no secret, this pre-dawn conversation was the first time I revealed my serious doubts about whether I could continue to work. By this point, nearly all my free time had devolved into scheduling medical appointments at top facilities in search of an answer.

I couldn't see the sunrise, but I saw the reflection of bright light on Kristin's bookcase, reminding me that my students would be at my door in minutes, so I got up to leave. I had become accustomed to the sideways looks due to my awkward movements. I noticed Kristin averting her eyes while I struggled to balance my body's weak trunk over even weaker legs. She escorted me to the elevator, and as the doors opened, my legs buckled. I hardly remember being led to the main office, buoyed by two colleagues, as long-time students looked on with concern.

Within minutes, an emergency substitute was called to cover

my classes. Within an hour, a colleague drove me home. Within a day, I knew I would never return to work. Not to collect my things. Not to say goodbye. Not to attend an event the community wanted to plan to honour my career. Instead, gifts for a much older person were delivered to my door—a beautiful wool blanket and a cookbook about "staying in," and heartfelt letters from more than a hundred students. Reading their personal notes of gratitude and well wishes, I felt dejected and fragile. Life as I knew it for two decades had come to an abrupt end as the reality of my deteriorating health finally collided with my fear of not being able to keep up with my beloved career.

Teaching high school English was an all-consuming calling; it provided me a sense of identity and channelled my passions, but it was also wearing me out. During too many lessons in my last few years, I slurred my speech and forgot key rhetorical terms for the college-level course I was so proud to teach. My physical decline started to take a toll on my confidence in the classroom as well. The anxiety made me shake as I addressed students I knew so well but whose names I couldn't recall. I struggled with vertigo on the stairs, and I fell in the hallways when in a hurry to beat the bell for class. Simple pivots around my classroom became dangerous; my legs often folded like a rag doll, and only at night's end did I remember the falls as I undressed and found my large purple bruises. And as my family turned out lights each night, I propped myself up with pillows in bed, my arms so weak they shook as I struggled to hold the pen and write legible feedback on student essays well past midnight.

In my final year in the classroom, I entered the school each morning nervous, afraid of the next time my body might let me down in view of hundreds of teens and my colleagues. I became very anxious, not just because of the ongoing steroid treatments prescribed to keep debilitating symptoms at bay, but the taxing mental acuity of preparing for work as well.

On an early fall morning, after a twenty-year career that put families and their students first, my body demanded I focus on the mystery surrounding my health. And with great clarity and some fear of what lay ahead, I finally listened. That first week after my final fall, I convinced my husband to sell our home and move out west for a fresh start. Maybe out west, I persuaded him on a walk after the trick-or-treaters had all gone home, I would have better luck getting a diagnosis, and even if I didn't, we would both reconnect with family and enjoy the natural wonder of the Pacific Northwest in whatever limited capacity I could.

In our new home in Central Oregon, I tried to remain hopeful that I would eventually be well enough to climb Mount Hood in the majestic Cascade mountain range. And in the meantime, while searching for a diagnosis, I took a Buddhism course to help me face the challenges life had thrown at me with renewed zeal. The instructor, Mary, led classes to help her "precious sangha" see the value of Buddhism in their everyday lives. And while I had never been and still do not consider myself religious, I enjoyed the in-person meditation and the empowering teachings until the pandemic hit and her class quickly moved online.

I tried a few times to attend Mary's classes online from home, propping myself up like I had done to grade essays, but my condition had worsened, and I was no longer able to sit up for the two hours in front of my computer for her teachings. When I stopped attending, something shifted in me and my world felt so much smaller. Here was one more thing my symptoms were taking from me. Mary had provided me with a weekly dose of such a healthy perspective, one that had given me a strong sense of agency, so it became increasingly difficult to handle the depression that resulted from watching even more of life move beyond reach.

Just before winter arrived, the mystery was solved as I was finally diagnosed with myasthenia gravis. My rare disease had been attacking what allowed my nerves to communicate with my muscles, rendering most of the muscles in my body too weak to function.

As the sun set earlier and earlier, my decline continued, and it became difficult to swallow and even at times to breathe, and I realized it had been easier to remain hopeful when I could keep my mind preoccupied in search of a diagnosis. Once I understood what I was dealing with, the reality of an isolating and challenging existence sunk in. I quickly realized that while living in Oregon was lovely, I was ill-equipped to accept the increasing physical limitations that kept me from daily functioning let alone hiking in the Pacific Northwest. I was still waiting to try an infusion regimen when I hit my lowest point.

As my back and neck struggled to hold me up, I was in bed that day before the sun went down. That night in particular I recall falling back on my bed, tears streaming silently down my flushed cheeks as I lay motionless. My hearing was muffled as the wonderful world faded away and the warm liquid puddled in my ear canals, rendering me cut off from everyone and everything.

Hours passed. The sky beyond my juniper trees faded from indigo blue to black as I thought about the roles in which I had previously thrived in my life: as a problem solver, a caregiver, a teacher, a mother. And then it hit me: For the first time it felt like I had lost all sense of autonomy. No self-help books, therapy, gratitude journalling, or meditation exercises prepared me to face the crushing depression. As the stars appeared and the moon lit up the snow outside my window, when there were no more tears to come, I remembered Mary and her offer to be there for us if we ever needed her. Instantly, I felt my weak facial muscles form a slight smile. I had one more lifeline, and I reached out the following day . . .

Dear Mary, I only stopped attending your classes online because I could no longer sit for your two-hour Zoom meetings. But if you have the time, I am really struggling with depression because of the decline in my physical health and would really like to talk to you. Since I have seen you, I have been diagnosed with a rare disease. Normally, I am quite pragmatic and optimistic, but I feel like I have tried all other options and nothing is working. As I wait for my first infusion next month, I am finding it more and more difficult to hold on to hope that my body won't reject it. I have not been able to use my legs, hold anything in my hands, or lift my arms, and I am now also struggling to swallow and catch my breath when I speak. As a result, too often, I have succumbed to crippling depression and even despair. In my darkest moments, I think of your teachings and am hoping you might make time to talk.

Mary responded quickly, and what transpired I appreciate now as one of the greatest gifts of my life. While I was stuck in bed, she offered to provide me with private teachings weekly via phone to accommodate me. The Buddhist teachings were transformative, and they spoke to me like nothing else had. I took notes when my hands allowed and asked questions when my mouth allowed. When I couldn't do either, Mary understood and guided me on a journey that challenged my perspective on life and my assumptions about what I could expect from it.

What I learned saved me. Mary didn't promise a saviour or a miracle, any false hope of recovery, or even an easing of chronic pain from muscle fatigue. Instead, her teachings gently encouraged me to accept several universal truths that address the nature of reality.

Incorrectly assuming I can expect to live free of health issues forever is born of ignorance. Decades of good health do not guarantee a future of good health, any more than the joy I found while teaching could last forever. After accepting the full truth about impermanence, I still had to own the harder lesson: I compound my psychological pain when I choose to invest energy into craving that my health be any different than it is. Mary encouraged me to analyze my thought patterns, and to this day, her sobering and empowering lessons guide me as I continue to embrace life with a rare disease.

Two years have passed since my diagnosis, and in that time, I have started life-changing infusions. Flares still occur, and when symptoms are especially bad, I still struggle. I admit it has been a long grieving process to accept that my body can no longer do the very thing I trained to do and that was so tightly tied to my identity.

The rhythm of my life has also changed, but I now find joy in the small moments that evaded the teacher who worked way too many hours and never saw a sunrise except through the rear-view mirror of my car in traffic during a long commute. Living with a disease that upends your life isn't easy, fitting in thirty-five days of infusions a year isn't convenient, but seeking moments of joy in my new life out west is a gift I am grateful for every day now. I have raised two Labrador puppies who I get to watch dive into the icy Deschutes River, I have found a love for plants and filled my home with them, and I have cherished the time I have been able to devote to reading books instead of grading papers.

My health has led me down a very challenging path, but I am so much stronger for it. And when symptoms hit me hardest, thoughts of the Buddha's Four Noble Truths buoy me.

For now, anyway, my health issues mean I cannot teach full time, but they also mean the adventures I'd hoped I'd take after my kids headed off to college are for now on hold as well. Instead of climbing Mount Fuji with my son, instead of visiting art museums in Spain with my daughter, instead of snorkelling in Mexico with my husband, for now, anyway, my dreams must embrace my new normal.

But what I have learned is more valuable than any round-trip international ticket: My mindset is always within my control, and there are always choices I can make. In fact, the further I get from my time in the classroom, the more honestly I reflect on it. Because my ego was fuelled by the rush of teaching students, I don't recall much else during those years. And ironically, all these years later, with many physical limitations that continue to wax and wane, I am making more personal choices that allow me to prioritize my search for peace and joy. I am connecting more frequently with my children, who live thousands of miles away, making new friends who share my love for dogs and reading for pleasure, and appreciating the sunrises and sunsets with my husband. But most importantly, I have found a way to coach a few students each season with their college essays, which allows me to still make an impact and work with teens. And finally, I can look back and see my career for what it was—an awesome chapter.

As I settled into a new life, focused more on gratitude than ever before, I reached out to Mary. We met for tea in Sisters, a very small town at the base of the Three Sisters mountains. We sat outside on a brisk spring morning, the sun shining on the snow-capped peaks. Steam rose from the ceramic mugs we tightly clutched to stay warm, and I thanked her for her teachings when I was so vulnerable.

Over the past few years, I learned to let go of having my identity wrapped up in being a full-time educator and the delusion that the joy I found in the classroom or my time there could last. Now, each day before dawn, I sit on the stone hearth of my fireplace, the heat radiating up my back, my two Labradors at my feet. We sit in the dark and I breathe deeply with anticipation and wonder as the sun begins to rise over the Central Oregon buttes: What colour will today's sunrise be? As the first gleam of light shines against the dark horizon, despite my symptoms, I am enthralled by the Aspen glow that bathes the sky in orange and pink. I say a silent prayer of gratitude for what this chapter has allowed me to learn and witness, and I am hopeful about what the next chapter might bring.

Kerri is living with myasthenia gravis.

Myasthenia gravis (MG) is a neuromuscular disorder primarily characterized by muscle weakness and muscle fatigue. Although the disorder usually becomes apparent during adulthood, symptom onset may occur at any age. The condition may be restricted to certain muscle groups, particularly those of the eyes (ocular myasthenia), or may become more generalized (generalized myasthenia gravis), involving multiple muscle groups. Most individuals with myasthenia gravis develop weakness and drooping of the eyelids (ptosis); weakness of eye muscles, resulting in double vision (diplopia); and excessive muscle fatigue following activity. Additional features commonly include weakness of facial muscles; impaired speech (dysarthria); difficulties chewing and swallowing (dysphagia); and weakness of the upper arms and legs (proximal limb weakness). In addition, in about 10 percent of patients, affected individuals may develop potentially life-threatening complications due to severe involvement of muscles used during breathing (myasthenic crisis).

https://rarediseases.org/rare-diseases/myasthenia-gravis/

Source : NORD

Kerri Mauer is a twenty-year veteran high school English teacher who designed the first media literacy unit for Maryland's Montgomery County Public Schools. Through a United States State Department program, she and her students hosted educators from Brazil and Europe, who learned about her approach for empowering the next generation to evaluate information that affects them, their communities, and the world. She was nominated by her community for the Washington Post Teacher of the Year in 2018. Kerry enjoys the local music and film scene, hiking in the Pacific Northwest, and coaching students across the United States with their college essays. She lives in Redmond, Oregon, with her husband and three dogs, Metolius, Levi, and Honeydew.

Kerri's chapter is dedicated to Mary Orton of the Central Oregon Dharma Center.

Chapter 21: Choosing Hospice, Feeling Alive

By Adrienne Shirk

I passed through the back door, my toe catching the threshold. My legs, along with many other muscles, had become impossibly weak over the past year, and catching my toe on anything and everything was an hourly occurrence. Off balance, I mindlessly stepped onto the patio, letting fresh air hit my tear-stained face. That day, at age forty-two, I'd become a hospice patient. A nurse had just left after completing an in-home intake. My choice was officially official.

In the United States, hospice is comfort care provided to terminally ill patients, particularly when active treatments no longer help or benefits no longer outweigh nasty side effects. My diseases had continued to progress through many powerful treatments for quite some time. I'd been so diligent with appointments, injections, and the mountain of pills I forced myself to swallow each day, but my body seemed set on decline—a sad but certain reality.

The main clinical qualification for hospice is that two doctors need to agree, in their estimation, you likely have six months or less to survive. The fact that my breathing, bladder, and digestion were all simultaneously failing made me a solid candidate, and severe pain tortured me daily. I had been very sick—hospital admissions, emergency room visits at odd hours, countless surgeries, and too many high-dose steroid tapers to keep track—for two insufferable decades. It was a life I hadn't expected, and the tireless self-advocacy I'd used to try to get to the bottom of it ultimately left me answerless. I was done putting every ounce of energy I had towards an increasingly impossible chance at remission.

Hospice was something my trusted team of doctors and I had discussed over the past five years. How could it not be? I fought multiple autoimmune diseases, survived a decades-long small bowel obstruction that caused severe malnutrition, even went into cardiovascular collapse (shock) in a matter of seconds during intravenous iron. I had survived CPR, received experimental infusions in intensive care, and developed a progressive, incurable neuromuscular disease no genetic test had explained but was nevertheless steadily stealing my abilities to move, urinate, breathe, and swallow.

I hardly felt dazed whenever providers could not hold back in vocalizing their surprise that I'd managed to stay alive. Now with hospice as my own reality, it felt vastly different from simply talking about it. Thankfully, hospice meant my pain could be managed using stronger medications, and no more specialist visits, tiring drives to crowded hospitals, midnight ER trips, invasive tests, or tediously long infusions either. Instead, hospice care was in-home, available any hour. That sounded all right to me . . . I was so very tired.

Though I knew without a doubt it was the right choice at the right time, seeing it through and having my official intake end only minutes earlier provoked emotion. I felt so many things at once but mostly disconnected and numb. I crossed our worn brick patio and shuffled around the yard. I craved the outside air in my lungs and the sun's warmth on my bare skin, in hope of becoming grounded. A biting wind whipped around me. Suddenly the thin T-shirt that had seemed like a perfect choice for unseasonably hot spring sunshine just hours before now felt woefully inadequate as it flapped around in an abrupt chill and oddly eerie light. I shivered . . . and my brain flickered online.

Oh right, the eclipse, I thought to myself, hoping I hadn't missed it. I scrambled inside, grabbed the special viewing glasses I'd stashed in our junk drawer, and dashed back out. Hugging both hands over my heart, I stood and glanced up—just in time for totality. How lucky! My whole life, I've always loved these sorts of moments: ones where you feel part of the expanse of the universe yet infinitely insignificant and small, all at once. I let this exact feeling wash over me. It began to wash away the numb . . .

That night, I posted a picture of myself during that exact moment to my socials. Friends immediately began sharing their thoughts:

"You're literally glowing." "This is such a peaceful picture." "The absolute joy in this one actually made me cry." I was flabbergasted they could sense this—and through an on-screen picture, no less! My group of friends, most of whom I had not yet disclosed my choice, could somehow sense the deeper spiritual significance of the moment from a single selfie. Words won't capture how this made me feel, but *awed* comes close. As each new comment appeared below the snapshot, I felt a growing sense that I was seen, understood, known, loved, and held—in ways God alone could.

I began to wonder if I should feel surprised by any of it. This connectedness, synchronicity, God-love with a capital *L* . . . these tangible, deeply spiritual phenomena never happen in a cluster without reason. They had been happening non-stop several days leading up to my decision, and they would continue in the weeks immediately following my hospice intake.

"I'm going into hospice care," I had told my best friend from nursing school nights before my formal intake was scheduled to occur. It was late. We were both texting from bed, thousands of miles between us but souls in perfect sync.

"I know," she had said. "I knew it. But I guess I was afraid to ask, because I already knew your answer."

I felt her love radiating to me, almost magically, alongside the glow of my phone.

"And I knew you knew, but it was still hard to even think about telling you, because I didn't want to cause you pain," I told her, laugh-crying at the loving irony as I typed, then tapped send. I felt a lump form, my throat beginning to clench tightly around it as warm tears suddenly flooded my cheeks, several detouring to drip off my nose onto my iPhone screen.

"We are so lucky our hearts are knitted together like this. SO lucky."

But these feelings of peace, joy, and connection had, of course, also brought with them a deep well of grief that begged me to feel it fully without pushing it away—much like opposites require the "other" to define their very meaning. My grief was so big it sometimes felt as though my chest would undoubtedly break in half with my next in-breath. Hospice grief is intense, and I'd never navigated anything like it.

I remember one particular morning, I felt overwhelmed I could no longer fulfill my role as caretaker for my partner and our dogs.

I started to cry. Then I couldn't stop . . . I sobbed so hard and long that I hyperventilated. I had no choice but to surrender to not being able to breathe well enough through my tears to get enough oxygen. I helplessly lowered my body onto our dusty, dog-hairy dining room floor. I stayed there for over an hour until my breathing regulated and I regained enough strength (and oxygen) to—albeit weakly—stand and continue my day. Deep despair, the heaviest grief, irreplaceable loss, boundless joy, transcendent peace . . . each took turns, and I had no choice but to let them all in, feel them, allow them to speak their truths to me, and then allow their release.

The morning after this meltdown, I decided to walk my favourite ridge to process my heartache. This trail had always felt like a cleansing, magical, holy place: a tree-lined ridge I often liked to walk alone, with a trailhead only blocks from home. It lazily zigzags up the entire side of a mountain and is one of those obscure, locals-only places where I have better odds of bumping into wildlife than humans. *Besides, who knows how long I can walk this trail before my disease makes it impossible?*

With the thought of that singular loss, plus the gravity of stopping active medical treatment to enter hospice suddenly hitting much deeper within my heart, I began to feel more and more consumed in worry with each step I took up the rocky incline. I was looking down, minding loose gravel and craggy outcrops while, admittedly, also deeply caught up in the many what-ifs my mind obsessed on while imagining my future on hospice. How long would it be, what might it look like, and just how much pain and suffering would I feel before I would . . . you know—all thoughts one shouldn't think yet can't help but dwell on in my position.

I was definitely immersed in this very deep, heavy "future-tripping" (as one sweet friend calls it) when my peripheral vision scarcely registered a tan-grey streak flash ahead of me on my left. I looked up in the direction of the blurry shape as a forceful westerly wind whipped around my face, deafening my ears to little else and stinging my eyes to the point of watering. I blinked back tears as fast as they formed in the corners of my eyes and strained to bring the blurry shape ahead into better focus . . .

A coyote?! Yes! It was!

He popped out from behind a still-leafless, scratchy shrub of very much the same colour and now stood in full view only ten feet away from me! We stared at each other while the pre-dawn light danced across us, gently illuminating our edges to each other in soft white-gold outlines. As the sun rose, there was nobody else for as far as my vision could absorb along the horizon before me and no sense of fear from either of us—it simply felt like mutual curiosity and a kinetic, connecting energy. We remained that way, motionless but undeniably synced with each other, for what felt like the longest time. I lost track of the existential health worries I'd been deeply fixated on only moments before, along with most everything else except the powerful energy exchange between me and this wild spirit.

After a while, I must've started to return to reality, as I abruptly reached for the iPhone stashed in my pocket. I fumbled with buttons and managed a very delayed, super crappy video. Despite my fuss, he didn't move an inch and continued to stand nearby and simply watch me. In the midst of the intense encounter, it wasn't lost on me that I could only lay claim to a pixelated iPhone video as "proof," but that made me all the more certain that what I was experiencing was actually much deeper than a cool photo or bragging rights. Standing there windblown while I paused on the ridge, I felt certain this was a deeply personal message.

Eventually, the coyote circled wide, then calmly dashed off below me, peacefully bounding through a sea of tall, scrubby grass dappled with first light. And I finally completely broke from my dream state.

When I felt my feet touching the earth again and sensed breath return to my lungs, all I could say was "Thank you Jesus, thank you Jesus, thank you Jesus." The whole of me felt like falling down on my knees, right there in the dirt, in complete reverence and spontaneous worship. No matter what your culture or beliefs, crossing paths with a coyote is not without profound spiritual significance. And it was poignantly clear this one carried a purposeful message from God, a tangible affirmation of my still-fresh choice for transition to hospice.

A gift amid grief—one of many to come, I would soon learn.

The very next morning, I was outside for yet another unseasonably warm day. One that was part of—for all us in wildfire country—a frighteningly windy, dry, and desperate stretch of weather. In response, I began tending to my early spring vegetable starts, even more generously watering a few raised beds where radishes were now growing rapidly. Despite the many serious risks the warmth posed, it had certainly done well to produce robust sprouts, flowers, and greens, weeks ahead of schedule. I poured cool tap water gently over my radishes, lost in the humbling wonder of witnessing any kind of new life (yes, even veggies), when I suddenly felt enveloped by intense buzzing.

I honestly couldn't tell where the buzzing was coming from, but as soon as my senses fully registered, it became louder. I felt like I was completely encased in a cloud of sound, vibration, and activity. The very next instant, I realized there was a swarm of honeybees all around me—so many, I couldn't even have counted. I felt calmly aware of their pulsating, magical energy connecting to mine in a peculiar yet thrilling way.

While I am by no means a honeybee expert (insect nerd, yes), I felt like this was really unusual bee behaviour; it seemed incredibly odd for them to swarm around me unprovoked and to ignore the ephemeral spring blooms that were plentiful nearby. Instead, they insistently attempted to drink from the damp soil in my planters. I stood, feeling equal parts confused and exhilarated. I observed them land repeatedly on my radish beds in particular, desperate to drink the water I'd sprinkled onto the soil. These bees were *thirsty*.

It took only a matter of minutes for me to construct a solution: a small Tupperware lid, filled with a few foraged rocks and topped off with more fresh, cool water. I set it down gently on one planter, then stood back and watched. They quickly learned that what they'd so earnestly been seeking, I'd just provided for them in abundance. Whenever their water became low, I filled it. And filled it, and filled it, and filled it. Every time I'd come by to check on them, they'd drunk it down again. Eventually, the bees were so used to me tending their little makeshift fountain that they'd hardly budge when I came by to refill. I could pet them, and after a few days of regular tending, I could even hold them as much as I wanted. To have their delicate, sticky little feet grasp my fingertip was wildly sweet and deeply moving every single time. After a handful of weeks and as many hard rains, the bees still visit daily, but in far less numbers, with far less urgency, and absent the pulsing intensity I'd first felt while enveloped in their sublime, golden swarm during the week of my hospice admission.

Caring for these tiny, needful bees, particularly during that week, became the daily, sometimes hourly, grounding routine I didn't know I needed, in what was an otherwise emotionally consuming, physically exhausting week of admin, home visits from many new caretakers, hospice team meetings, and a whole lot of phone calls. The metaphors I discovered in caring for these bees—incredibly—reflected back to me my own increased needs, inadequacies, raw vulnerability, and newly intensified fears.

Would I be able to just as fully and humbly trust all the new sets of hands who were going to be helping *me*? Would *I* stay open to God's presence—His supernatural arms wrapping around me—even when it arrived in unexpected forms? A dense honeybee swarm . . . wordless encouragement while crossing paths with wildlife . . . or friends showing they knew and loved me deeply without me even having to ask.

Could I give myself permission to freely feel gut-wrenching levels of fear and grief in this hospice process, but also keep my heart equally open to the energies of abundance and connection? Could I trust that this major life change, one that would inescapably bring loss (both energetic and emotional) and scarcity to my life, might actually also hold demonstrable love, fullness, and provision?

Could I?

Repeatedly, in the days leading up to my intake, during that first week on hospice, quite often in my very own backyard, and even still to date, God undeniably keeps showing me "yes."

There are countless other equally serendipitous stories I could spin about the magic and comfort I felt during that week. I think it would take an entire book to do them all justice, but it might honestly prove impossible to distill all my wonderfully deep, spiritually affirming experiences from powerful felt-energies into mere words.

When medical treatments and medical providers fail us—as rare disease patients—does what we initially feel register as opportunity, joyfulness, connection, or light?

Hardly.

But the week I officially transitioned from active treatment to hospice was one of the most spiritually energizing, beautifully rich times of my entire life. And I think that's a sentence most people wouldn't expect to *ever* read concerning end-of-life care. I'm here to tell you that, at least for me, it's veritably and powerfully true. What a wonderfully strange situation that my hospice transition was a time I felt so vibrantly alive, even as the word *dying* was being used increasingly to describe me.

I've often wondered how many people might feel the same if confronted with my prognosis. I don't know how to explain any of this outside of my spirituality, so I think it's best left shared and appreciated rather than mentally dissected. But I also deeply hope, however exceptional my process or experiences may seem, that anyone facing a similar decision can be comforted and soothed in reading about mine.

Unmatched experiential highs accompanied my grief in every moment surrounding my hospice enrollment—they very much *still* do. And nearly every time I catch myself feeling uneasy or scared, drowning in my own tears, or feeling terribly alone, something or someone *always* comes to comfort me and show me the Holy in it—often in the very next moment. Prior to my hospice decision process, God had never before used so many people or animals—definitely never coyotes and swarms of bees—to so tangibly wrap me in His embrace, so clearly affirm my choices were right for me, or so tenderly let me know I was going to be okay.

Thankfully, most days now I feel more awed than afraid.

I might be dying, but I've also never felt so joyful, loved, whole, or alive.

Adrienne is living with a multitude of conditions including undifferentiated connective tissue disease with prominent features of Sjögren's syndrome, autoimmune autonomic neuropathy, non-dystrophic myotonia, chronic neuromuscular respiratory failure, and idiopathic inflammatory myopathy.

Undifferentiated connective tissue disease (UCTD) is a rare autoimmune disorder. Patients present with the features of different connective tissue diseases, including systemic lupus erythematosus, systemic sclerosis, polymyositis, and rheumatoid arthritis.

www.ncbi.nlm.nih.gov/pmc/articles/PMC10350301/

Source: National Library of Medicine

Autonomic neuropathy occurs when there is damage to the nerves that control automatic body functions. It can affect blood pressure, temperature control, digestion, bladder function, and even sexual function.

https://www.mayoclinic.org/diseases-conditions/autonomic-neuropathy/symptoms-causes/syc-20369829

Source: Mayo Clinic

Myotonia is a rare condition where your muscles aren't able to relax after they contract. Myotonia disorders are classified as dystrophic or non-dystrophic. Both of these disorders affect the electrical process that regulates muscle contraction.

https://my.clevelandclinic.org/health/diseases/22334-myotonia
Source: Cleveland Clinic

Chronic respiratory failure is a common complication of many types of neuromuscular and chest wall disorders. A patient with otherwise normal lungs can develop respiratory failure through muscular weakness and/or thoracic cage abnormalities.
www.annualreviews.org/docserver/fulltext/med/74/1/annurev-med-043021-013620
Source: Annual Review of Medicine

Idiopathic inflammatory myopathy is a group of disorders characterized by inflammation of the muscles used for movement (skeletal muscles). The primary symptom of idiopathic inflammatory myopathy is muscle weakness, which develops gradually over a period of weeks to months or even years. Other symptoms include joint pain and general tiredness (fatigue).
https://medlineplus.gov/genetics/condition/idiopathic-inflammatory-myopathy/#:~:text=Idiopathic%20inflammatory%20myopathy%20is%20a,can%20occur%20at%20any%20age
Source: MedlinePlus

Adrienne Shirk graduated from Millersville University with a bachelor of biology and athletic and academic honours. Ten years later, she returned to school and acquired a bachelor's degree in nursing at Villanova University via a fourteen-month accelerated second degree program. Despite multiple personal academic and athletic accolades, however, her proudest accomplishment has been helping female student-athletes, which she returned to Millersville as an alumnae to do, volunteering daily as a mental skills coach for over six years.

Adrienne also loves spending time in nature, photographing animals and plants while strolling on local trails, and going for walks with her dogs. She also enjoys bird and insect identification and taught herself to knit four years ago when a mentee became pregnant and she wanted to support them. When she has the energy, she posts online about the simple and beautiful joys she sees in everyday life on her Instagram @summerof_24; however, since going under hospice care, she has limited energy to interact and prefers you email her at bird8brain@gmail.com.

Adrienne grew up in Lancaster County, Pennsylvania, though she is currently out of state after pursuing specialized medical care that she was unable to access in her home state.

She dedicates her chapter to her hospice physician, Dr. David Wensel, DO, who has helped guide her in a safe and holistic way.

Welcome to *Positively Rare* Chapter Chat

In this book club–style section of *Positively Rare,* you will find questions related to each chapter of the book. These questions have been written by a professional social worker from HD Reach, Erika Boulavsky, LMSW, LCSW. She has written these questions as a means of prompting conversations about the complex issues we face in the rare disease community.

Ways you can use this section of the book:

- Members of a support group can each be provided with a copy of the book. A chapter is chosen to be read each month. People read the chapter on their own and then discuss the questions at the next meeting.
- A story can be read aloud at a support group meeting, and everyone can discuss the questions at the meeting.
- An individual can read the stories and ask themselves the questions independently.
- Families can read the stories together and discuss the questions.
- Medical professionals can read the stories and discuss them with their team.

Thank you for taking the time to read this book and to be a part of this journey.

Erin Paterson, project coordinator and developmental editor

About Erika Boulavsky

Erika Boulavsky, LMSW, LCSW, serves as the community outreach specialist for HD Reach, a non-profit that provides educational and supportive services to the Huntington's disease community. She is responsible for building relationships and education within the medical community, reducing barriers to care, and overseeing supportive programs for HD families. Erika has a BA in sociology from Coastal Carolina University and a master of social work from the University of South Carolina. She is originally from Myrtle Beach, South Carolina, and began her journey as a social worker for her local hospice agency before getting involved with HD Reach. She resides with her wife and two dogs in Raleigh, North Carolina. She met her wife within the Huntington's disease community, and both have family members affected by Huntington's. They have been long-time volunteers, board members, and speakers for various HD organizations.

Chapter Chat Topic Guide

The stories in *Positively Rare* cover a wide range of topics and issues written by people impacted by different rare diseases.

To help you navigate this book, we have included a list of some of the rare diseases and topics covered in each chapter. The stories are so complex that they touch on many issues, but we have listed the main themes of each story. Some of these may be sensitive topics and triggering for some people.

If at any time you need support, please know you are not alone. Many local associations are available to assist with your needs or offer a listening ear. For an international list of local resources, please visit globalgenes.org (https://globalgenes.org/mental-health-and-well-being).

Some of the more common topics in this book include advocacy, caregiving, diagnosis journey, depression, finding community, genetic testing, grief, medical crisis, medical procedures, medical trauma, suicidal ideations.

Chapter 1: The Birth of a Dragon Mom

By Laura Will

1. Can you think of a time in your life where you were made to doubt your gut reaction or professional opinion? Did you end up being correct about the situation? How did it feel when you were finally believed?
2. The author describes the exact details of her experience when given a diagnosis: Memorial Day weekend, ginger ale and saltine crackers, the smell of sanitizer. What kinds of events within your own life stick with you to the point you can recall every specific detail?
3. "Medicine had just labelled our child a deformity." What emotions were evoked when you first read this line? In reading it again, how could this harsh reality impact this child's and his parents' lives?
4. Did you know of polymicrogyria prior to this story? Did this chapter help you learn about this condition, especially through the eyes of a parent?
5. "Despite my education and empathy, I had subtly internalized societal prejudices of disability as a sad or diminished aberration of the 'normal' human experience." This is a raw and honest moment of reflection. Does the author help you reflect on your own internalized prejudices? What are some actions we as a society should be taking for disability communities?
6. "I still had to learn that disability rights are, quite simply, human rights." What emotion did this powerful statement evoke from you when you read it?
7. "Expectations about the child Alden was supposed to be, expectations I had not even realized I had, came unbidden into my mind." We all have some level of expectation for how our lives should have turned out, or sometimes the "what ifs." Can you recall an expectation that you needed to let go of, adjust, or grieve?

8. After reading this story, what words would you have for the author?

Chapter 2: The Perfect Mother

By Courtney Wells

1. The author did her own research and was ignored by the doctor when presenting the Beighton scale. Does the doctor's reaction make sense? In what ways did the author have to advocate for herself?
2. What does the author mean when she says, "My joy and triumph could not resurrect the part of me who died in that terrifying emergency department on Halloween night"?
3. How does the author lose autonomy? How important is personal autonomy to us individually?
4. The author acknowledges that she "never regained the feeling that my body belongs wholly to me." Why is that?
5. Throughout the author's journey, she states that "the most devastating loss I've suffered is the sociable person I used to be." She recognizes that people in her life began to drift away. Why do you think some people drift away when a friend's health is affected?
6. It is predicted that the author will be wheelchair dependent by the age of fifty. How would you cope with this knowledge?
7. What did the author learn about being a "perfect mom"? How did her journey change her behaviour?
8. This chapter describes the author's detailed experiences and her dedication to get home to her family. She ends the chapter by expressing her fight to stay with them. What is the most common theme throughout?

Chapter 3: We Are All Advocates

By Daniel DeFabio

1. After Lucas's diagnosis, the family goes to an art museum, and the author reflects on Lucas's reactions to recycling a cup: curiosity and joy. He mentions that these reactions helped him make future medical decisions for Lucas. The author states: "Are we allowing for more joy in, for, and from Lucas?" What does this question mean?
2. The author details that one of the symptoms of Menkes syndrome is brittle hair, but the health care team did not recognize this telltale sign in Lucas. He acknowledges that this is why "newborn sequencing is so important for so many rare diseases." What does he mean by this?
3. What are some of the milestones and experiences the author was concerned his son would not get to experience? How did they end up differing from those that were imagined?
4. How is grief recognized throughout this chapter?
5. The author states: "I can't honestly say how much of this was to busy myself into distraction and how much was motivated by a feeling that something had to change." What is the author referencing? Have you ever found yourself busying yourself with distraction, or being motivated by a sense of something needing to change, or both?
6. The author uses the term *imposter syndrome*. What was he referring to? Was this helpful, or did it hinder the author? In what ways have you, if ever, experienced this?
7. How has the author taken his own experience and used it to help others with rare diseases?
8. Is it true that we are all advocates? Has this chapter redefined the word advocate for you?

Chapter 4: Seeing My Future Through Caregiving

By Erin Paterson

1. The author lists the ways she is currently caring for her dad. In what ways does she advocate for him?
2. The author explains how communicating with her father may result in responses sixty seconds later. Would you have the patience? If not, how would you work on that if this was your own loved one?
3. "Staff are too impatient to wait for a response and often label him as non-verbal." How does this misinformation impact the author's father?
4. "I know he walks sort of funny. That is his normal gait," I told her. "I realize it might not look safe, but that is the way he has been walking for a long time, and we are okay with the risk." What is the author doing in this part of the chapter? Why is the family okay with the risk?
5. "Is it a need of my dad's or a need for the staff, who don't want to do their jobs?" How does the author provide examples around this?
6. What is it like for the author to know her genetic status of HD while caring for her father with HD? Does this add complexity to caregiving?
7. How does the author cope with receiving phone calls about her father? Why did she have difficulty purchasing new pants for him?
8. How does the author illustrate balancing depression, grief, self-care, and giving in to emotions without being consumed? Why does she feel guilt?

Chapter 5: A Walking Rarity

By Tessa Koller

1. How do art and writing help the author throughout her journey?
2. The author acknowledges that her mental health plays a large role in how she navigates her continued health issues. Based on your own experiences, how powerful do you feel the importance of strengthening your mental health and support has been?
3. "Now is not my time" is what the author repeats when going to the hospital during her health crisis. How does "Now is not *my* time" have a different impact than "Now is not *the* time"?
4. The author details her external resources and internal resources. What are your external and internal resources?
5. How has the author coped with living with chronic illnesses? Did this happen overnight or take time to develop?
6. What portion of the author's journey is most memorable to you as the reader?
7. Do you feel it is important for individuals like this author to share their experiences to help educate others? What parts of the chapter do you relate most to within your own life?
8. How has advocacy become a large part of this author's life?

Chapter 6: Perseverance and Hope with a Rare Illness

By Joe Kammers

1. Within the chapter, the author recalls when he was seeking answers and people would tell him "It's probably all in your head." How did this make the author feel? What could have been more helpful for him to hear from his peers?
2. The author states: "I wanted the pain to stop so much that I considered hurting myself, but I could not because of the support of my family." What kind of support do you think the family provided to the author during this time? What are ways to support those experiencing chronic pain, fatigue, and lack of answers?
3. The author's insurance changes multiple times throughout the chapter. Each time, he must seek out a new clinic and a new neurologist. Does this have any positive benefits, or does this delay his journey to answers and treatment? How differently did each neurologist treat the author?
4. The author had previously been misdiagnosed. What are the different ways he had to advocate for himself before and after?
5. At the children's hospital, a member of the health care team stated: "I never thought I would ever meet someone with your version of this disease, so this is a great opportunity to learn from you." Did the author feel supported and welcomed by this? How would this make you feel?
6. The author won free IVF treatments from a radio station by entering a video and testimonials. What are some ways you have heard others find access to afford IVF?
7. As the author is adapting to life with his daughter, he acknowledges "dreading not being able to keep up with her as she gets older." His wife assures him that their daughter "will learn to understand." Are children quick to adapt and learn about their surroundings? What words of reassurance would you give to this author?

8. The author's superpower is "persistence." What are the ways the author was persistent throughout his story? How can persistence be included within your own story?

Chapter 7: One Step at a Time

By Kimi Sorensen

1. In the beginning of the chapter, the author acknowledges that her life seemed normal when she was young, and hydrocephalus did not feel like it was part of their lives. Their mother states, "You may not even need the shunt anymore. They will probably never take it out, but who knows." Can you imagine yourself in the author's parents' shoes? Do you see yourself taking a similar pathway in allowing the author to enjoy childhood, or would you see yourself trying a different approach?
2. The author describes feeling lucky for her childhood and guilty at the same time. Why is that? Do you have any experiences of feeling lucky and guilty simultaneously?
3. After surgery, the author experiences a stroke. What helped her work through the aftermath of the stroke?
4. The author describes the difficulties of having a stroke at age seventeen. Think back to when you were seventeen years old. In what ways would that have impacted your own life? How different would your life be?
5. The author states she was never an emotional person: "I've always been more of an 'if this is going to be the way it is, I'll figure it out and move on' type of person." She acknowledges that after fifteen years, she allowed herself to grieve. What was she grieving? How does one give themselves permission to grieve?
6. How has hydrocephalus been a motivator in the author's life?
7. What can come from the chain reactions of this author's experience and now career stemming from hydrocephalus? Do you think this gives the author a perspective within her career that others may not have?
8. What was the overall theme of this chapter? What stood out to you the most?

Chapter 8: Excited to Be Growing Old

By Andy Sinclair

1. After the transplant, the author's body is now able to "create and use its insulin within a few weeks." In what ways did this help the author?
2. After the author had a seizure in front of her boss, she admits she worried about her job because her boss had seen her "vulnerable." How did this event impact the author's worries about the future?
3. What kinds of challenges came with receiving the transplant? Were any of the examples provided shocking to you as the reader?
4. The author mentions being able to sleep "without fear of not waking up" after her transplant. If you have not had this concern, can you think of how one copes with such a fear?
5. How can the eye specialist tell when the author has been sick?
6. The author talks about the advances in health care and treatments. What are some mentioned within this story that stood out to you?
7. The author states, "Had I been born one generation ago, I would not be one of the lucky ones." Again, by reinforcing the advancements of health care, the author acknowledges her mortality had those advancements not been made. What has this chapter taught you as the reader? How has it affected you?
8. It is revealed that donor islet cells come from someone who has passed away. How does the author honour the family and their loved one? What would you do to honour the family and their loved one?

Chapter 9: We Are All Connected by Rare Diseases

By Maddie Gillentine

1. How has the author broadened your knowledge of autism spectrum disorders and rare disease research?
2. How did Will's diagnosis help him understand his own identity?
3. In what ways did the author's brothers influence her choice of career?
4. How is social media utilized within this chapter? Can social media help rare families connect with each other?
5. According to the author, why is it important that "researchers see the disorders they are researching"?
6. Does this chapter provide any reassurance around the advancement of research?
7. How did starting the HNRNP Family Foundation create a ripple of change and community?
8. What did you learn the most from this author's chapter?

Chapter 10: Our Story Begins

By Erika Boulavsky

1. Why did the author view being able to understand her grandmother's speech as a superpower?
2. Thinking of today's generation, how has the culture shifted around communication with children? Would you say there is more honesty, or are there still barriers around difficult topics such as illness and death?
3. How pivotal was it for the author to be asked to keep the family secret? How did this affect her journey into the future?
4. In the family, who took the first step of talking more about Huntington's disease with others? How did that impact the rest of the family? Was this a positive or negative action?
5. In the author's story, what is bittersweet about her journey of being impacted by HD?
6. Why do you think it was important for the author to tell her story at the convention? How did this help her?
7. What is the HD Parity Act, and why is this important for those with HD? Could this have a ripple effect for other bills?
8. What could be some future complexities in Erika and Melissa's relationship, with both being impacted by HD?

Chapter 11: Two Journeys Become One

By Melissa Ryant

1. How important has communication been for the author and Erika? Why was it important to maintain communication throughout the story?
2. What are some of the ways the author fell into a caregiver role when young for her mother? What was her brother's role at the time?
3. After testing gene negative, Melissa says, "The flood of emotions I felt in that moment—and have felt ever since—was like holding two conflicting truths simultaneously. How could I be just like my mom and also not have HD? How could I feel relief along with an overwhelming sense of guilt? I continue to hold these two truths to this day, and balancing them can be harder on some days more than others." Have you ever been in a situation where you felt like this? Does this give you a better understanding of what survivor's guilt is?
4. What is the importance of the term *ohana* to the author? Do you have a similar type of chosen family within your own life that supports you?
5. The author says that HD is "a family disease." Explain what she means by that, using examples from the story.
6. Why doesn't Erika want to test for this genetic illness, according to the author? Why is this a complex decision for individuals? Overall, would knowing you are at risk for Huntington's affect how you view your life and your future?
7. How has the HD community helped Melissa and Erika's relationship?
8. How can you use Melissa's story as a lesson for your own life? What part do you feel made the most impact on you?

Chapter 12: Embraced by a Bond Built Beyond Sacrifice

By Halsey Blocher and Heather Halsey Dye

1. The author contrasts "run-of-the-mill choices" with choices about life-saving medical procedures for a child to help provide a picture of the vast differences in decisions a parent might need to make. What kind of perspective does this provide to you as the reader?
2. "Peace in this kind of choice is more like letting go than being right." Can you relate to this statement? What experience in your life put you in a position like this, if any?
3. "Everyone said it was going to be so cool to be taller. No one told me how far away the floor would suddenly become." This was just the beginning of Halsey's new journey; what other challenges did she experience after her surgery?
4. Halsey states that her mother "redirected my focus away . . . calmed me down . . . Most importantly, she kept me from falling. She would never let me fall." Through Halsey's perspective of her mother keeping her safe, who is or was that person for you? Through Heather's lens, who do you keep from falling—literally or figuratively?
5. What have you learned from Halsey and Heather about resiliency?
6. Halsey acknowledges that her interdependent relationship with her mother is "different from what the world often considers 'normal'" and that society tells her she is "too old for this and it's time for me to be less reliant on her." Does society embrace reliance on others? How can this story help empower others or help others empathize with diverse experiences?
7. "Spiritual wellness, hope, faith, and positivity are the treasures to be found amid the bond of caregiving." If you have experienced being a caregiver, what are your "treasures" found from caregiving?
8. What parts of Halsey's and Heather's story impacted you the most?

Chapter 13: The Struggles of Being a Caregiver

By Hannah Remillard

1. The author became a young caregiver for her mother and started managing her family's finances at fourteen years old. Can you think of what you were doing at fourteen years of age?
2. Why was it difficult for the author to relate to people her age?
3. As her mother's driving became a concern, what did the author do to maintain their safety?
4. How did the mother–daughter relationship change throughout the chapter?
5. The author writes about her mother's behaviours before and after medication. What are the pros and cons of taking this medication?
6. In what ways did the author struggle to talk and relate with her peers?
7. How was the author affected by grief and depression?
8. What was the last straw before burnout for the author? How did her family adjust to her need for change?

Chapter 14: My Unforeseen Transition from Nurse to Patient

By Jen Cueva

1. What are some of the ways the author coped with her illness throughout the story?
2. Do you feel the author's knowledge or experience as a medical professional (nurse) played a role in the decisions she made after diagnosis?
3. Think about when the author mentions not being in control. How does one adapt from being a nurse to experiencing day-to-day life as a new patient?
4. What strengths did the author gain after her PH diagnosis?
5. The author reveals that people with her condition usually live for three to five years. You later learn this story was written almost twenty years after her diagnosis. How did that make you feel?
6. What has this author's story brought to your life?
7. How did family and community help the author's journey?
8. What would you say is the overarching theme of this chapter?

Chapter 15: A Decade of Diagnosis, Depression, and Dreams

By Kelly Kearley

1. The author describes having to wait eight months for her child's results. How do you see yourself coping for eight months awaiting this diagnosis if you were in the author's shoes?
2. How do you feel about the process by which the author received the genetic results? (Receive diagnosis by mail; follow up with genetic counsellor/geneticist the following month.) Do you feel genetic results should be mailed to a home, or should the results be reviewed in person with a genetic counsellor/geneticist (or neither)? What do you think would give you the most support, personally?
3. "So, you are going to start grieving now" is what the geneticist stated when the author was leaving with her son. What are some ways someone can grieve while their loved one is still alive? What are your experiences with grief?
4. The author provides some examples of statements other parents have said to her while she was in the midst of "turmoil and suffering" after her son's diagnosis. What are some statements, actions, or questions that may have been more supportive during this time, if any? Does the author help you reflect on your reactions and self-awareness when interacting with others going through turmoil?
5. "I had always believed that if you worked hard, you could achieve anything. However, this had just 'happened,' and I wasn't prepared for the lack of control." Do you feel we can ever be fully prepared for life? Do you resonate with the author's words? Can you recall the experience that revealed this to you, if you do?
6. The author acknowledges that her journey "would become one of acceptance" but that at the time, she was not ready for that. Do you feel there is a timeline for accepting your

circumstances, or should that be an individual journey? Does this look different for everybody?

7. "Speaking to someone and putting my emotions into words made them lighter and gave me the ability to release them. Counselling gave me permission to feel. It helped me to understand my reactions and take back control of my emotions." If you have experienced counselling, how did the experience affect you (negative or positive)? If you have not experienced counselling services, does the author's description help provide insight in a way you have never heard before?
8. "You can't control the cards you are dealt, but you can control your reaction to them and how you build your life around it." How can this advice be used within your own life?

Chapter 16: Finding Joy Through the Trauma

By Jenny Jones

1. At the beginning of the story, the author uses the term *medical trauma*. How does the author go on to provide examples of the medical trauma she experienced?
2. How does the medical trauma the author experienced as a child impact her as an adult? Does it have long-term effects on her view of life?
3. In what ways did the author seek community? Did these communities provide any support to her?
4. The author discusses feeling "wronged" by her parents and doctors as she provides details about her procedures and how those around her would react. What feelings did this evoke within you when reading?
5. The author states: "I've wanted to die since I was nine; I've viewed my life ever since as being repeatedly robbed of death. I was supposed to have died, more than once." What did the author actively do to work on her mental health?
6. What does the author's story teach you about self-care?
7. Can joy be unreachable? How does the author obtain joy?
8. What part of this story felt relatable to you personally? What do you take away that you can include within your own life?

Chapter 17: An Ordinary Life with Morquio

By Jocelyn Wong

1. What kinds of difficulties did the author experience as a child with disabilities in China?
2. What differences did you learn between Chinese and American cultures?
3. In what ways did health care change over the years throughout the author's life?
4. The author moves to the United States at the age of eleven years old to live with family—entering a new country, with extensive medical needs, and starting within a new educational system. Was this a positive or negative experience for the author?
5. What words would you use to describe the author and her journey with Morquio?
6. How does this author's story empower you?
7. How did the author benefit from connecting with others impacted by Morquio?
8. How is resiliency displayed in this chapter?

Chapter 18: A Man in Crisis

By Dunstan Nicol-Wilson

1. How does the author describe the impact of sickle cell anemia on his identity?
2. The author gives insight into his experience with the health care system. How does his treatment reflect broader societal issues? Do you have experiences with the health care system where you have not felt safe or felt ignored?
3. The author recalls happy moments from his childhood being disrupted by sickle cell crisis. How does this continue to impact him throughout adulthood? How different would your own childhood be if you had a chronic illness as described (pain, sick days from school, doctor appointments, crisis after enjoyable moments)?
4. What coping mechanisms did the author develop to deal with his pain and crisis? How effective were these in the short term? In the long term?
5. How does the author's mental health evolve throughout his journey?
6. The author mentions the racial stigma and biases he faced within the health care system. How does this compound the challenges of living with a chronic illness? What steps can be taken to address and reduce racial biases in health care?
7. How has vulnerability affected the author's personal and social life? In what ways can vulnerability be a source of strength?
8. What kinds of lessons did you learn from the author's story around chronic illness, health care, racial stigma, and personal growth? How can these lessons inspire your approach to your own life or to supporting others?

Chapter 19: I Am a RAREsie Warrior

By Joanne Paquette

1. The author recalls her interactions with Dr. Denis Desjardins versus other doctors. What was it about Dr. Denis that stuck with the author all of these years about his presence?
2. How did the author find independence at a young age? What transformed her?
3. How determined was Dr. Denis to help, with limited to no information on the author's condition?
4. Recall the incident that happened when the author was in the hospital for three months. How did the health care team's lack of attention forever impact the author?
5. At what age did the author start drinking alcohol? Why was this a "getaway" for her?
6. How did the culture of Quebec in 1972 negatively affect the author's care at the time?
7. The author wrote that "at times I think I complain for no reason." What would you say to her if you could?
8. How did a lack of community affect the author's coping and impact her parents?

Chapter 20: Finding Sunrise

By Kerri Mauer

1. Within an instant, the author is no longer able to continue her career as a teacher. In your current career or previous careers, how would you have coped with such an abrupt end?
2. The author starts to enjoy in-person meditation classes. The pandemic started and the class was then moved online, making it more difficult for the author to engage in the practice. How did she adapt to this?
3. The author reflects on previous "roles" within her life. How have your roles adapted and changed over the years?
4. The author mentions feeling like she had "lost all sense of autonomy." This led to her reaching out to Mary for support. Can you think of a moment in time where you needed to reach out to someone for support? What made you take that next step?
5. Impermanence essentially acknowledges that nothing lasts forever and that change is inevitable. Does this bring you comfort or create discomfort? Why?
6. When the author had to give up teaching, her life looked very different from what she had envisioned. What are some things she actively did to get to where she is today?
7. "My mindset is always within my control, and there are always choices I can make." How does this resonate with you? Do you believe your mindset is within your control?
8. What is your identity tied to? How do you see yourself?

Chapter 21: Choosing Hospice, Feeling Alive

By Adrienne Shirk

1. "That day, at age forty-two, I'd become a hospice patient." Can you remember the thoughts and immediate feelings that arose in you when reading this line for the first time?
2. How has hospice care been beneficial for the author? Do you have any experiences within your own life of hospice? If not, do you have an understanding of what hospice is, or did you learn more through this chapter?
3. "I've always loved these sorts of moments: ones where you feel part of the expanse of the universe yet infinitely insignificant and small, all at once." The author is experiencing the eclipse immediately after her hospice intake. Can you think of a moment you have experienced where something so significant made your worries and fears seem far away or at a distance for a short period of time?
4. For you as the reader, what piece of this author's journey has made a profound, lasting memory? What will you take from this story into the future with you?
5. In reading, did you find yourself immersed in the author's grief? Does the author provide a raw and honest view of her experience to you? Did this chapter reveal a new perspective around death, dying, and grief?
6. What was your reaction to the author's encounter with the coyote? How would you react? Would this be a powerful experience, or would you feel differently?
7. "I might be dying, but I've also never felt so joyful, loved, whole, or alive." In reading this sentence, does it provide any form of reassurance to you about the inevitable? What do you hope your experience will be when it is time?
8. How do you think this chapter will impact others who read it? How can readers carry on the legacy of this author?

Acknowledgements

First and foremost, thank you to all the rare disease warriors in this book who had the courage to step up and share their stories with the world. You have done an incredible thing! It has been an absolute honour getting to know you. My life has been enriched by working with you, and I know that will be the same for each person who reads your stories.

Each writer came to the project with a message they wanted to share, but it was more than that. One thing that connected us all together, other than rare disease, was the desire to help others in our rare disease communities. That's you, the reader.

I hope you found a connection with the words written in this book and that these stories have enriched your life as well. Whether you learned about a new rare disease, envisioned a new life post-diagnosis, or used these stories to inspire your research, we are so grateful you took the time to read them. Thank you for your compassion and understanding.

Further thanks is extended to Jamie and Jacklyn from Be Do Have Movement, who played a pivotal role in this book's coming to life. Not only is their company, Be Do Have Movement, the premier sponsor for the book, they believed in the project from the start and have been guiding me every step of the way. They have also graciously supported our writers on their journeys.

A big thank you as well to Erika Boulavsky, Jessica Fein, and Daniel DeFabio, who have added their professional expertise to the book.

Special thanks to all our sponsors and donors:

- Be Do Have Movement
- HD Reach
- Apex Social
- PTEN UK and Ireland Patient Group

This truly was a collaborative book, and we couldn't have done it without you!

Sponsor Resources

This book would not have been possible without the generous support of our sponsors. We are so grateful you believed in this project. Thank you for helping us make a difference in the lives of people in the rare disease community.

Premier Sponsor

Inspired by our personal journeys, we built a father–daughter coaching business to help other people step into their "something more."

> Jacklyn: "I left the advertising world because settling for a career that affected my mental health wasn't worth it."
>
> Jamie: "I started on a new career path in my fifties because my job was no longer bringing me joy."

Together we co-founded the Be Do Have Movement, a business and life-coaching company dedicated to transforming lives. We empower individuals to embrace their potential, take responsibility for their happiness, and pursue their dreams with courage. Our mission is to support those who seek more from life, creating a ripple effect of positive change—one person and one dream at a time.

We offer memberships for monthly personal growth training, programs for real estate agents looking to holistically elevate their lives and incomes, and private coaching for people who want personalized plans to transform their lives.

It all begins with YOU. Listen to that little voice in the back of your head telling you that you deserve to follow your true dreams.

www.bedohavemovement.com

Access your complimentary virtual gift bag from the Be Do Have Movement and Lemonade Press Inc.

https://www.bedohavemovement.com/lemonadecommunity

Supporting Sponsors

apexsocialgroup
Developmental Childcare

Since 2008, Apex Social Group has provided specialized live-in child care tailored to nurture development and unlock each child's potential. Their care professionals, with backgrounds in education, therapy, or health fields, help create supportive routines and integrate therapeutic homework into daily life. Apex care professionals are experienced in caring for children with autism, ADHD, cerebral palsy, and more.

https://apex-social.com

Reach is a North Carolina–based 501(c)(3) non-profit working to improve the care and quality of life of those affected by Huntington's disease. Founded in 2009, HD Reach provides connections to medical providers, referrals to local services, care management, family support, education, and anonymous genetic testing.

www.hdreach.org

Supporting Sponsors - Continued

The PTEN UK and Ireland Patient Group's purpose is to improve the lives of patients, parents, and carers of all ages, in the United Kingdom and Ireland, who are affected by PTEN genetic alterations. This rare disease is thought to affect around 300 people in the UK, although the exact number of patients identified is not known.

The patient group's official charity objectives include providing better patient support, increased awareness, more accurate and accessible information, earlier diagnosis and intervention, greater research into treatment and prevention, and improved coordination of care. Our first, and priority, mission is to support all those affected by this rare disease. We do this through providing useful resources on our website, annual patient meetups, patient grants, and our PTEN counselling service. We work and live by the motto "together we are stronger."

Help Make a Difference

We put together this book because we felt the stories of people in the rare disease community needed to be heard. We wanted to help take away the stigma of living with rare diseases. Most importantly, we wanted people to know they are not alone.

If you think this book will assist someone else, here are a few ways you can help:

- Write an online review on Amazon, Goodreads, or Indigo. Or wherever you purchased this book.
- Take a selfie with the book and tag us on social media. Better yet, email us a picture.
- Tell your friends and family about the book.

Thank you so much for taking the time to read these stories and for helping spread awareness for rare diseases.

To find out more, visit https://lemonadecommunity.com.

Instagram @lemonadepressbooks

About the Publisher

At Lemonade Press we believe everyone's voice deserves to be heard. We work with under-represented medical communities to create specialized anthologies about different medical conditions and rare diseases.

We take people who are not writers and coach them through the storytelling and writing process to create captivating personal stories geared towards inspiring their community.

Our books change people's lives by helping them control the narrative of their journeys, reducing their fear of living with a disease, and connecting them with others who share their experiences.

After publication, 50 percent of the proceeds from book sales are donated to a related charity. The chosen charity for this book, *Positively Rare*, is Global Genes.

Lemonadecommunity.com
Instagram @lemonadepressbooks

Also Published by Lemonade Press

All Good Things: A Memoir About Genetic Testing, Infertility, and One Woman's Relentless Search for Happiness

Huntington's Disease Heroes: Inspiring Stories of Resilience from the HD Community

Bloopy the Alien Learns About Huntington's Disease

Made in the USA
Middletown, DE
19 November 2024